THE THAI RESISTANCE MOVEMENT
DURING WORLD WAR II

JOHN B. HASEMAN

SILKWORM BOOKS

ISBN 974-7551-62-4

This edition first published by Silkworm Books in 2002

Silkworm Books
104/5 Chiang Mai–Hot Road, M. 7, T. Suthep, Muang,
Chiang Mai 50200, Thailand
E-mail address: silkworm@loxinfo.co.th

Typeset by Silk Type in Garamond 11 pt.
Cover photograph: Seri Thai troops, Bangkok, 25 September 1945
Printed in Thailand by O. S. Printing House, Bangkok

CONTENTS

Appendices

LIST OF MAPS & FIGURES

MAPS

PREFACE

I want to express my appreciation and thanks to Khun Trasvin Jittidecharak, director of Silkworm Books, for recognizing the importance of the subject of this book and for improving the production quality. The many people who participated in the Thai resistance movement made a significant contribution to Thailand's freedom and independence after World War II. My particular thanks to Ms. Susan Offner, who edited the work and transformed it into the professional product you are reading. Silkworm Books did yeoman service in correcting the spelling and transliteration of the Thai names. Nevertheless I may have made errors in the spelling of Thai names, in my efforts to recognize the contributions of as many people as possible in the resistance movement. Those mistakes are my responsibility and I apologize for any errors.

This book first began many years ago, as the thesis for my Master of Military Art and Science Degree at the U.S. Army Command and General Staff College. My classmate, then-Captain Sanchai Buntrigsawat, Royal Thai Army, encouraged my interest in the Seri Thai and provided the initial bibliography of Thai language sources. John E. Taylor, Modern Military Branch, Military Archives Division, U.S. National Archives, gave of his time during the Christmas holiday. My gratitude to personnel at the Orientalia Division, U.S. Library of Congress, for their prompt reply to my requests for materials. Mr. Gene P. Wilson, Information and Privacy Coordinator, Central Intelligence Agency, was most courteous in providing portions of the official history of Office of Strategic Services activities in Thailand. Dennis F. Quigley, a good friend, helped in obtaining other materials.

The United States Army Command and General Staff College, Fort Leavenworth, Kansas, provided the time and research facility to prepare the draft academic study. Dr. Ivan Birrer encouraged the scholarship that I hope is contained herein. I owe thanks to my faculty advisors, then-Lieutenant Colonels Lucien Clawson and George McQuillen, and Dr. Sidney Klein (Colonel U.S. Army Reserve) of California State College, Fullerton, for their help and encouragement.

I owe special thanks to persons associated with the Center for Southeast Asian Studies, Northern Illinois University. They provided me with research materials not available elsewhere in the United States. Later, they encouraged me to transform the original thesis into a monograph for publication. Dr. Donn V. Hart, Director, encouraged the development of this work. Dr. Clark D. Neher and Dr. M. Ladd Thomas, Department of Political Science, gave freely of their knowledge and experience. I am grateful to Mrs. Arlene Neher for taking time from her own busy research to assist me. My thanks also goes to Professor Lee S. Dutton, Director, Southeast Asia Collection, Northern Illinois University Library, who guided me to new sources in the collection. Professor Peter Ananda, Director of the South/Southeast Asia Library Service, University of California Library, Berkeley, furnished additional research materials.

Finally, I owe a great debt to my family. My parents, Colonel and Mrs. Leonard L. Haseman (now deceased), first encouraged me to put my thoughts on paper. They, and my six brothers and sisters have always supported my efforts, and it is to them that this book is respectfully dedicated.

John B. Haseman

INTRODUCTION
TO THE FIRST EDITION

Many aspects of Thai political history are unique. Thailand was the only nation in South and Southeast Asia to remain independent during the long period of Western colonial rule from the seventeenth to the twentieth centuries. Even so, it was very much shaped by the unequal treaties imposed by Western powers. While China and Japan were also subjected to unequal treaties, their experience in many ways was decidedly different due to their larger territory and population size as well as their secular Confucianized culture. In contrast, Thailand was perhaps the first sovereign nation in Asia to learn that much of its internal political and economic development was closely tied to the forces and vagaries of the external environment. It was one of the first Asian nations to learn how to compromise portions of its national interest and to accommodate international influences.

Thailand's experience in World War II was another phase of this unique and distinctive history. During this global conflict between the Allied and Axis powers, no other nation, large or small, was in its unprecedented status. Thailand was attacked and occupied by Japanese military forces, yet it retained its political sovereignty and a largely autonomous government throughout the war. It had a monarch living abroad and a populace overwhelmingly opposed to the Japanese presence. Yet Thailand did not follow the example of Belgium, Holland, or other Axis-occupied countries and establish a government-in-exile. The Thai government declared war on Great Britain and the United States, yet Thai nationals in Britain and America were never interned by either of the Allied governments. Instead they were soon co-opted into an effort by the British and American military services to assist the removal of Japanese troops from Thai soil.

This monograph by John Haseman is an endeavor to explore an important part of Thailand's experience in coping with Japan's Greater East Asia Co-prosperity Sphere during World War II. It is a very commendable work seeking to throw light on another unusual phase of Thai political history which has received insufficient attention by either Thai or foreign scholars. It consists essentially of a description of the organization, structure, operations, and problems of the Thai resistance movement during the war, based on both English and Thai language sources. The study also utilizes unclassified information provided by the Office of Strategic Services (OSS) and the Department of State, although much official documentation on this period is still unavailable for academic research. Very important, this work profits from the warm and sincere enthusiasm of the author for its particular subject matter.

The merits of this monograph are many. Beyond the chronological description of the resistance movement in World War II, it depicts many characteristics of Thai politics which transcend the brief time span of four short wartime years. It shows many elements which continue to influence Thai public policy today. It likewise explains some of the important qualities of the international environment surrounding the Thai kingdom.

One significant contribution of Mr. Haseman's study is to clarify some portions of the role of Phibun Songkhram as the top military and government leader throughout most of the war. This effort may assist in destroying some myths about Phibun which have persisted for many years. Some observers of Thailand during this period have labeled the Thai wartime leader as something less than a genuine nationalist and depicted him as a "collaborator" or "puppet" of the Japanese. Others have wondered why Phibun was not tried as a war criminal at the end of the war and was instead allowed to go free. Many persons have likewise questioned why Phibun was able to emerge as the prime minister again in 1948, a feat which made him the first "pro-Axis dictator" to regain power after the demise of Nazi Germany, Fascist Italy, and Imperial Japan. Perhaps the most perplexing has been the question as to why after 1950 Phibun was able to make such a quick rapprochement with the United States which had played the major role in defeating Imperial Japan, while Pridi and many Free Thai leaders active in the wartime resistance movement against the Japanese were ousted from power within a few short years.

The answers to these fascinating questions are obviously complex. Only fragments are offered in the author's pages. Yet this monograph shows that in spite of many shortcomings as a leader, Phibun was a genuine Thai nationalist in a delicate position who used his political authority as much as possible to mitigate the harshness of the Japanese occupation and to protect the Thai people. This was shown in the author's coverage of Phibun's instructions to Seni Pramoj prior to his departure to serve as the Thai minister in the United States. Phibun clearly explained that Thailand's foreign policy was not pro-British, pro-Japanese, pro-American, or "pro-anything" other than pro-Thai. This point could be profitably restated for observers and analysts of Thai politics in the post–World War II period. It would answer the frequent question whether or not Thai foreign policy has been "pro-Western," "pro-American," or "pro-communist." In spite of the flexibility in Thai foreign policy, its basic goal, regardless of the personal status of the top political leadership, has always been the survival, security, independence, and welfare of the Thai nation.

Haseman also explains that Phibun was frequently forced to take certain unpopular actions as the early wartime prime minister because he really had no viable alternatives. A good example was Phibun's decision to order the cessation of fighting by Thai troops against invading Japanese forces in the first few days after 8 December 1941. Within the course of a few hours the Thai prime minister was informed that Japanese troops were attacking Thai territory by land and sea from bases in French Entocone. He was told again that Thailand could expect no military assistance from either of the major Allied powers, Great Britain or the United States.

In this situation Phibun had no realistic choice but to make some accommodation with the Japanese and to try to maximize the freedom of action for his government and the Thai people.

During the war Phibun took other actions which showed a high level of responsibility for the welfare of the Thai kingdom. When he realized the Japanese were losing the war against the Allies, he tried to move the capital of the country to the northern province of Petchabun. On the surface this effort appeared foolhardy, yet it was an attempt by Phibun to establish a military and political base away from Bangkok and the heavily populated central plain where he could possibly wage guerrilla warfare against the deteriorating Japanese position in his country. Also, when Phibun learned of the formation of the clandestine Free Thai organization inside the country by his archrival Pridi, he placed no obstacle in its development. In many ways he facilitated the gradual integration of his own administrative, police, and military services into the ranks of this anti-Japanese underground. The prime minister could have easily hampered the actions of the Free Thai apparatus inside the country by his own counter-measures or by exposing it to the Japanese. Instead he did neither. The withholding of any suppressive action enabled the Free Thai organization to make its great contribution to the Allied war effort and to assist in the rapid rehabilitation of Thailand in the eyes of the major Western powers in the early postwar era. In a strange and indirect manner, Phibun probably warrants some credit for this important accomplishment.

Another salient characteristic of Thai society depicted in portions of this study is its commonly cited status as a "loosely structured" social system. Numerous social scientists, Thai and foreign, have used this term to describe the Thai class structure since it was first used by John Embree in 1951. The author of this monograph explains how many elements of the Thai government and the Thai resistance movement against the Japanese in World War II fit this classification. In places the portrayal of this highly flexible and fluid quality of Thai collective behavior arouses a feeling of pathos and a touch of humor. It shows both the genius and the nadir of Thai politics. At times it also makes one wonder how the Thai nation has survived and succeeded as well as it has.

Phibun himself revealed some of these attributes on the opening day of World War II by purposely absenting himself from Bangkok and taking a tour of the border provinces at the very time his government was expecting an attack from the Japanese military forces in French Entocone. A short time later Pridi purposely went into hiding so he could avoid signing Phibun's declaration of war against the United States and Great Britain and thereby qualify himself as an ardent spokesman of the document's "illegality" at the end of the war. In Washington, D.C., Seni Pramoj stretched the Thai political style even further by publicly stating that the declaration of war by his government did not represent the will of the Thai people. The Thai minister to the United States never explained to the cooperative Americans how he made this determination, and he conveniently overlooked the important fact that the Thai people had few opportunities in their highly authoritarian society to register their choice of a government. Seni did even more. As an unabashed royalist who deeply regretted the overthrow of the absolute monarchy only ten short years before, he nonetheless helped form the Free Thai movement in the United States which eventually joined the Free Thai organization inside Thailand established by Pridi Banomyong who was the leader of the 1932 coup which had abolished the absolute monarchy. Seni and Pridi soon worked together to rid their country of the Japanese presence through the Free Thai movement which they both claimed was "the real representative of the Thai people."

The author explains many other aspects of the "loosely structured" society and political behavior in Thailand. He shows, for example, how the Thai method of utilizing top-level personnel often appears confusing and contradictory, yet at the same time it does achieve an important and rational purpose. Early in the Japanese occupation, Phibun dismissed Pridi from his Cabinet as the Minister of Finance, but he appointed Pridi as the regent for the absent monarch thereby assisting Pridi's efforts in organizing the clandestine Free Thai movement inside the kingdom. Phibun also removed Pridi's close associate, Direk Chaiyanam, as the foreign minister, yet Phibun promptly appointed Direk as Thailand's ambassador to Japan, a position used later to provide the Free Thai organization and the Allied governments with information on military and political conditions inside wartime Japan. The military attache in the Thai legation in Washington, D.C., Colonel Khap Kunchon, was sent by Phibun to keep an eye on Seni, yet both Seni and Khap soon worked closely together in the Thai resistance movement against Phibun and the Japanese. And in the final year of World War II the overt members of the Free Thai movement in front of the Japanese military authorities ousted Phibun as prime minister by a negative vote in the National Assembly. Little wonder that foreign observers then as now are frequently baffled and dumbfounded by many aspects of Thai politics. Yet somehow the system works and it continues to achieve one of the most impressive records in promoting economic and social modernization in Southeast Asia.

To American and British readers, this monograph has a special appeal in its description of the important contribution made by the Thai resistance movement to the Allied war effort and the eventual defeat of the Axis powers. Information obtained by the Free Thai organization was especially significant in the war against Imperial Japan since General MacArthur refused to permit the Office of Strategic Services to establish intelligence or paramilitary operations in the Pacific theater. Much of the information on the Japanese war effort obtained by the Free Thai apparatus during the last year of the war was consequently one of the major sources of intelligence available to the American and British governments during this crucial period. This information included data on military targets for Allied bombing raids as well as reports on the effectiveness of these air attacks.

The contacts of the Free Thai organization with the Thai embassy in Japan provided important information on political and military conditions inside wartime Japan as well as reports on the damage caused by American bombing missions against the Japanese main islands. The first raid by B-29 bombers against military targets in Japan was based on information supplied by the Free Thai organization. A Free Thai agent with close contacts inside the Japanese military command in Bangkok obtained valuable information on Japanese troop movements which were subsequently attacked by American and British aircraft. In addition to useful military intelligence, the Free Thai organization procured information on the location of Allied prisoner-of-war camps in Thailand. The Free Thai movement also assisted in the escape of many American and British pilots shot down on Thai territory.

For analysts of Thai politics in the post–World War II era, this study provides interesting data on many members of the Free Thai movement who subsequently assumed important positions in the Thai government. In most cases these future leaders got their first taste of political and administrative power during World War II, and often it led to a distinguished career in public service. Puay Ungphakon, who eventually became the governor of the Bank of Thailand and rector of Thammasat University, was active in the Free Thai organization in Great Britain, and near the end of the war he was infiltrated into Thailand by parachute to assist in intelligence gathering operations. Net Khemayothin who served as a plans officer for Phibun and a liaison officer for Pridi during the Japanese occupation played an important restraining role in the struggle for power after the war between the civilian leaders affiliated with the Free Thai movement and the new military faction headed by Colonel Sarit Thanarat and Colonel Phao Siyanon. Thanat Khoman, who later became the Thai ambassador to the United States and the foreign minister (from 1958 to 1971), received some of his early diplomatic experience in the Free Thai organization in the United States. Thawi Chunlasap was a liaison officer between the Free Thai underground in Thailand and the British High Command in Ceylon, and in 1945 he assisted American air crews in precision bombing attacks against key Japanese targets in Thailand. Thawi subsequently became a top commander in the Thai Air Force and served as a confidant to Field Marshal Thanom Kittikachon. Following the overthrow of Thanom's military regime in October 1973, he formed his own political party and won both a Cabinet post and a seat in the National Assembly in the April 1976 elections.

Perhaps the most important contribution of Haseman's monograph in a political context is its portrayal of the most extensive and unified political organization ever formed by the Thai people to achieve a common purpose. In considerable degree it shows a brilliant achievement in what political scientists call "interest aggrega-tion." The ranks of the Thai resistance movement during World War II were filled with great diversity in education, wealth, political orientation, and social class. It included royalists, conservatives, liberals, radicals, princes, commoners, judges, bureaucrats, police-men, students, and peasants. These different types of people worked together in a common cause which stretched organizationally from Washington, D.C. and London to Ceylon, China, Japan, and many provinces in Thailand. For four years they forgot or submerged their personal differences and worked together successfully in an effort to remove foreign troops from their native land. Without realizing it, they overcame the frequently cited limitation of the Thai people that they do not work well together in large numbers or in a large organization. In effect, the Thai resistance movement in World War II established the high-water mark of political unity and effective-ness in recent Thai history. This standard has not been matched in the monotonous internecine feuding, political divisions, and mili-tary coups of the postwar era. Very likely, this wartime record of political cooperation and concord will not be approached again for at least several decades.

The author is well aware that his study does not comprise a com-plete coverage of this significant period of Thai history. In his concluding pages he cites many areas not described in this mono-graph. These include the role of the Chinese Nationalist intelligence organization inside wartime Thailand, the operations of Chinese agents in the British and American intelligence services, the role of Christian missionaries in the resistance movement, and the personal accounts of Thai resistance leaders written in the Thai language. He might have added that much useful information on these aspects of his topic is available and could be obtained from personal inter-views with many Free Thai leaders still living in Thailand.

A significant need in the study of Thai history during World War II is to relate the Thai resistance movement to broader developments affecting the institutions, leaders, and organizations of the Thai political system. Such an effort would require an expansion of the focus from essentially military history to political analysis and assessment. It would be more difficult and demanding, yet it would undoubtedly produce greater insights and knowledge. It would give a much better understanding of the characteristics of Thai politics after World War II. It would explain, for example, some of the reasons for the total lack of ideological struggles within the Thai resistance movement during the war, in sharp contrast to the bitter ideological conflicts in wartime resistance movements in Vietnam, Laos, Cambodia, China, Korea, and Indonesia. It would explain some of the reasons why the Free Thai movement grew from small personalized factions around Seni and Pridi into a vast impersonal bureaucracy stretching across wide continents and oceans. It would likely explain how Thailand in considerable degree was an early barometer of the forthcoming demise of Great Britain as a major power and the impending emergence of the United States as an international superpower.

Yet this monograph is a good start in the right direction. The research provides much information and answers many questions in recent Thai history. It thereby arouses a desire for more information and the answers to more questions in this important field. Hopefully, the author and others concerned about these same questions will continue in this worthy endeavor.

Frank C. Darling

AUTHOR'S INTRODUCTION

The anti-Japanese resistance movement in Thailand is a little-known aspect of guerrilla operations during World War II that has been largely overlooked in English-language histories of the war. This book examines the Thai resistance movement and its contributions to the people of Thailand during its short four-year history. I cover the formation of the resistance movement in the United States, England, and Thailand; the difficulties of communication and coordination during its early years; the organization of the fully established resistance movement; and the support and assistance provided to the Thai by the English and American intelligence agencies.

I limited the scope of the book to keep the study to a manageable size. For example, the internal and external political situations that exerted heavy pressure on Thailand and the resistance movement during the period under examination are discussed only briefly. I provide some basic analysis and evaluation of the resistance movement in the greater context of international politics. This is not, however, an examination of the political history of Thailand during World War II. The examination of political events is limited in this monograph to matters that exerted heavy pressure on the resistance movement, its leadership, and the movement's potential for political advantage in a final settlement of Thailand's position after the war.

The nature of the subject made research difficult. Most English language accounts of the Thai resistance movement are extremely general in nature and lack the detailed information necessary for effective research. Official documentation is either scarce or still classified. I was able to make only limited use of the documents of the Office of Strategic Services (OSS) and the U.S. State Department. I relied extensively on Thai language accounts of the resistance movement for necessary details. It should be recognized that the relative scarcity of such materials required considerable emphasis on a small number of Thai authors. Fortunately, additional members of the resistance movement, many of whom went on to distinguished careers in politics, business, and the military, have recently written memoirs which contain mention of their role in the World War II resistance movement.

While I mention the political climate in Thailand immediately prior to the outbreak of hostilities, the bulk of the book examines the organization, structure, operations, and problems of the Thai resistance movement. Unfortunately, I could give only light treatment to one major aspect of the Thai resistance movement: the substantial role of Thai Christians and foreign missionaries, particularly in northern Thailand. However, the difficulty in assembling necessary source materials hampered efforts to do justice to the substantial contributions this group made to the Thai resistance effort. This is a fertile area for further research.

The terms "resistance" and "resistance movement" are used interchangeably to refer to the entire anti-Japanese effort. The cadre, civilian, military, and police elements taken together form the resistance movement. This usage equates to the U.S. Army official definition of resistance movement, that is:

A. A resistance movement is an organized effort by some portion of the civil population of a country to resist the established government or an occupying power.

B. A resistance movement generally is composed of a hardcore resistance leadership, clandestine element (underground), overt military element (guerrilla force), and a supporting civilian population (auxiliary). The full development and eventual success of the resistance depend on the ability to mold these component elements into an efficient and effective organization.[1]

I depart somewhat from regular military terminology in the use of the term "underground." Thai sources and I use this word to refer to the resistance leadership element as well as to the guerrilla forces organized in the later stages of the war. The terms "guerrilla force" or "guerrillas" refer to that paramilitary organization specifically created to conduct armed operations against the Japanese forces in Thailand.

The Thai names are written according to the Royal Institute system of transliteration. A full transliteration of Thai names used in this study is in the final appendix. There are a few exceptions to this rule. For Thai officials who changed their names, I use the more common name. Furthermore, some major Thai figures prefer to use a particular spelling of their names and such versions are in common use. For example, Marshal Phibun is referred to in this form since he almost never used his full name, Plaek Phibunsongkhram. Similarly, Pridi Banomyong used this name during his years of leadership rather than his titled version, Luang Pradist Manudharm.

The Thai resistance movement played a crucial role in determining Thailand's postwar history. Continued independence and sovereignty for Thailand was by no means a foregone conclusion as Allied leaders planned postwar political strategy. The resistance movement and its record of assistance to the Allied effort in Southeast Asia was a primary reason why Thailand gained American support in its struggle to maintain its national sovereignty.

I have used this book to present detailed information on the political and military role of the Thai resistance movement. Making extensive use of Thai language materials, I examine the organization and functions of the resistance movement and its key leaders. The first edition of this book was the first English language work available to the general public to outline the details of early attempts to contact the Allies, both by the pro-Japanese government as well as resistance movement figures. It also was among the first such works to cover Allied attempts to infiltrate Thailand with Thai agents trained by Western intelligence agencies. I used information from both Western and Thai sources to present as thorough an examination as possible of the infiltration and operations of those agents.

This second edition corrects a few errors pointed out to me over time, and also provides a more consistent transliteration and spelling of Thai names. Though many people have assisted in making this edition as accurate as possible, there may still be unintentional errors. I apologize and take full responsibility for them.

CHAPTER ONE

POLITICAL AND MILITARY DEVELOPMENTS LEADING TO WORLD WAR II

POLITICAL BACKGROUND

In 1941 Thailand was a quiet yet apprehensive country. World War II had started two years earlier in Europe, while Japan's Pacific empire had conquered much of East Asia. Thai leaders, whose nation was the only Southeast Asian country not colonized by a European power, observed with concern as the Axis developed. France, England, and the Netherlands were either overrun by invading German forces or hard pressed to survive. The Thai, surrounded by colonial possessions ruled from Europe, observed with concern as neighboring countries became involved with their European masters in the war.

The British-ruled countries of Burma and Malaya formed Thailand's southern and western borders. The French Indochina territories of Laos and Cambodia, already dominated by Japan, bordered Thailand on the east. Other countries in the region also owed allegiance to Europe: Ceylon, India, Singapore, Hong Kong, and the Netherlands East Indies. Geography alone suggested that Thailand could not remain untouched by the war. To land-starved Japan burdened with war costs in China and Manchuria, Thailand's surplus rice was a tempting asset.

Thailand always has been fiercely proud of its history of national sovereignty, and its ability to maneuver among the major colonial powers in the region while remaining independent is well known.

The country had not hesitated to exercise a local version of balance-of-power politics to preserve its independence. In retrospect it was reasonable to expect that Thailand would pursue the same political maneuvering in the shadow of World War II.

MARSHAL PHIBUN'S POLITICAL DOMINANCE

Thailand politically approached war with a new internal system of government untested in international affairs. Less than a decade before, the 1932 coup d'etat had abolished the absolute monarchy and replaced it with a constitutional monarchy. The new system, although democratic on first view, was in effect a personal dictatorship under the prime minister, Field Marshal Phibun Songkhram.

In the aftermath of the 1932 coup d'etat the Thai military moved rapidly to fill the psychological and political void formed by a major change in the government. Phibun led the military faction of the "Promoters" who overthrew the traditional system of Thai government. Pridi Banomyong, a brilliant liberal economist, led the civilian faction. While the two men and their supporters had cooperated during the 1932 coup d'etat, as time passed the military and civilian factions moved farther apart. By 1938 the military had gained almost unlimited power and Phibun's accession as the prime minister marked the end of effective civilian leadership. Pridi and several of his supporters remained active in the government but overall civilian influence in governmental affairs declined rapidly. The decades of struggle for leadership between Phibun and Pridi are an intriguing element of modern Thai history.

Phibun as prime minister and Pridi as minister of finance were the most dominant figures in the Thai government. The two men and their respective supporters automatically considered the impact on internal political powers of all major decisions and changes in Thailand. The approach of World War II was no exception. Events that surrounded the decisions by Phibun concerning wartime policies, and the formation of the Thai resistance movement to oppose those policies, must be considered in the context of the personal power status of the two giants of the Thai political scene.

Phibun believed that totalitarianism was the ideological wave of the future. Germany and Japan were dominant powers in the world, while Western-style democracies appeared weak and ineffectual.[1] Phibun had no qualms about embracing a dictatorial philosophy with military strength and nationalism as its cornerstones. He felt that strong dictatorship was the most efficient way for a developing country to achieve progress. Donald E. Nuechterlein has described Phibun's philosophy of leadership:

> Phibun was determined that Siam must break out of its backwardness and achieve a larger role in Asian affairs. [He] looked to Germany and Japan . . . as models for Siam's future.[2]

Japan was more than willing to extend friendship to Thailand. Thailand's geographic and political position in Southeast Asia, and the bounty of its agricultural economy, were not overlooked by Japan's leaders. Japan took an overt step toward gaining Thai favor by supporting Thailand's claims for portions of French Indochina. The support climaxed on 11 March 1941 when the two countries signed an agreement returning to Thailand two enclaves in Laos and much of northwestern Cambodia. This action gave Thailand control of the entire west bank of the Mekong River above Cambodia, which had been part of Laos, as well as much of Battambang province in Cambodia. It was the first major step in the process by which Thailand became indebted to Japan.

As 1941 drew close to the fateful month of December, Prime Minister Phibun found himself and his country drawn closer to the Japanese orbit. He seemed alert to the nature of the Japanese threat to Thailand but was powerless to act.[3] His awareness was demonstrated in part by his last minute requests for military equipment and arms to both the United States and England. But by late 1941 neither of these two countries had the capability nor the inclination to help Thailand.

THE JAPANESE ULTIMATUM AND INVASION OF THAILAND

In late 1941 the Thai National Assembly, perhaps realizing that the country was threatened, took several steps to resist the growing power of the Japanese and to assert some degree of determination. As early as September 1941 the National Assembly passed laws curtailing the number of Japanese who were entering Thailand ostensibly as tourists but in reality as advance military cadres. Thai troops were sent to the Indochina border where Japanese troops had massed in both Laos and Cambodia. The National Assembly also passed a law that made it the duty of all Thai people to resist any invasion with arms, economic power, or any other means, including destruction of crops and animals to prevent their capture and use by an enemy.[4]

Throughout the first week of December 1941 officials in Bangkok grew more certain that Japan had embarked on a policy to enlarge the war. High-level discussions in the Thai Cabinet speculated over the action Thailand should take either to counter Japanese expansion or to coexist with it. Virtually every knowledgeable official agreed that Japan was certain to attack the British and Dutch colonial territories in Southeast Asia. Thai officials also agreed that Thailand had no chance to conduct a successful diplomatic or military defense against Japanese military forces if Japan decided to attack their nation. Discussions in the Cabinet therefore centered on the complex issue of Thailand's options in the areas of coexistence and on the preservation of Thai sovereignty and independence.[5]

Mom Ratchawong (M.R.) Seni Pramoj later recalled Phibun's description of Thailand's foreign policy in the text of a statement released in the United States:

> Before I left Bangkok on my mission to this country . . . I asked the Prime Minister point-blank to tell me what was the foreign policy of Thailand. Were we pro-Japanese, pro-English, pro-American, or pro-anything? He replied that we were not pro any other country in particular. We were pro-Thailand.[6]

4

This statement indicates that Phibun was determined to maintain independence no matter what actions he might have to take. Phibun was later described in terms ranging from patriot through traitor, but a review of events leading Thailand into World War II shows that he had at heart the best interests of his country and people. On 7 December 1941, at 10:30 P.M. (all times and dates cited are Thailand time) the Japanese ambassador to Thailand told the Thai foreign minister, Direk Chaiyanam, that Japan had declared war on the United States and England. He further informed the Thai minister that Japan did not consider Thailand to be an enemy country. However, he "requested" the right of passage for Japanese troops through Thailand into Burma and Malaya. He stated that such permission would be taken as a sign of friendship. Despite the late hour the Thai Cabinet was meeting to consider the increasingly dangerous situation facing Thailand. The Japanese ambassador actually called Direk out from the Cabinet meeting to hand him the Japanese note. The initial Japanese "request" was summarily rejected by the Thai Cabinet.[7]

On 8 December at 2:00 A.M., less than two hours after the attack on Pearl Harbor, Japanese forces began landing in Thailand.[8] The Fifth Division, Twenty-fifth Army, landed at the cities of Pattani and Songkhla and on the island of Ko Samui in southern Thailand. The Guards Division, Twenty-fifth Army, landed small elements at Samut Prakan at the mouth of the Chao Phraya River south of Bangkok. The bulk of the Guards Division entered the country overland from Cambodia at the town of Aranyaprathet.[9]

Prime Minister Phibun was not in Bangkok when these events occurred. He was on an inspection trip to military camps in eastern Thailand and western Battambang province and was therefore not available to make decisions. In his absence nobody had the authority to pass orders to Thai military and police forces. Considering the crisis facing Thailand and the rest of Southeast Asia, Phibun's absence from Bangkok at such a momentous time could not have been by accident. Apparently Phibun was trying to avoid or postpone making any immediate decisions on Japanese demands. In any case, he designated the deputy prime minister, Police General Adun Adundecharat, to preside over the Cabinet but did not give

General Adun the power to make final decisions affecting Thailand's national security.

In the confusion of the situation and because of poor communications with the South, it was some time before the Thai Cabinet realized the seriousness of the situation. While debating the Japanese demands, the Cabinet received word of a second wave of Japanese landings at Chumphon and Prachuap Khiri Khan along the Kra Isthmus.[10]

Thai forces fought with courage at Songkhla and Pattani, while levels of fighting varied elsewhere.[11] Simultaneously with the landings, hundreds of Japanese military agents surfaced in uniform throughout the country to guide invading forces to pre-selected objectives and routes of advance.[12] By the end of 8 December the Japanese had secured positions at Songkhla, Pattani, Ko Samui, and Hat Yai in the far south. While they had also established positions at Chumphon and Prachuap Khiri Khan, additional units had effectively surrounded Bangkok. (See map 1.)

General Adun and Foreign Minister Direk had some leeway in stalling the Japanese because Phibun had not delegated to them the power to make decisions. However, with the success of the Japanese military landings this advantage was lost. The Japanese ambassador was increasingly insistent on a reply to the note. He was not inclined to countenance further pleas that only the absent prime minister could reply to Japanese demands. Intense pressure on the Cabinet resulted in lively discussions. Some ministers, including Pridi, argued for at least a token show of force to allow the situation to develop further before capitulating.[13] Others argued for an immediate end to the fighting on the grounds that it was futile to waste Thai lives in a cause that could not be won. Phibun's supporters generally espoused the latter argument.

Prime Minister Phibun hurried back to Bangkok when word of the Japanese invasions reached him by telegram at Aranyaprathet. He arrived at the Cabinet meeting at about 7:00 A.M. on 8 December.[14] The remainder of the meeting was an excruciating conflict between Thai national pride and the military realities confronting the country. At issue was not only the nature of the decision on a policy with Japan, but also the issue of Thai sovereignty. Not all accounts of this Cabinet session have been published, but some facts are available.

General Adun briefed Phibun on the situation and the extent of the military conflict. Direk explained the details of the Japanese demands and the choices they offered Thailand. Adun presented a convincing case for Thailand to seek the best situation possible since no other country would be able to assist Thailand. News of Japanese successes at Pearl Harbor and in the Philippines, refusal by England and the United States to send aid to Thailand, and the Japanese inroads in the country were overwhelming. Japan had demonstrated that its forces could defeat the great powers and that its troops could easily crush Thailand if ordered to do so. Adun concluded that it was better to surrender to the Japanese demands rather than fight a hopeless and costly military battle that would result in Thailand being completely conquered.[15] Despite fervent statements of Thai pride by the Pridi forces in opposition to these proposals, Phibun's supporters carried the issue. At noon on 8 December Phibun ordered all Thai forces to lay down their arms, arguing that it was futile to fight to the death.[16]

There are some postwar historians who hold that Phibun insisted on an immediate cease-fire to depict himself as a hard-line Japanese puppet, leaving others free from the taint of making that decision. From a practical viewpoint the decision is defendable. The cease-fire saved thousands of Thai lives and spared the people further destruction of their cities and farms. A senior Thai officer who studied in the United States immediately after World War II supported Phibun's actions:

> Phibunsongkhram was one of the most influential personages who did all they could to stop a Japanese invasion. . . . When the Japanese actually came with their weight of armor, and Siam could not be saved by war alone, Phibunsongkhram negotiated with the Japanese with the view of saving Siam and avoiding the destruction and misery which might befall the Siamese people.[17]

Taking the opposite view, a long-time supporter of democracy in Thailand has commented:

Map 1. Japanese Invasion Routes into Thailand, 7–8 December 1941

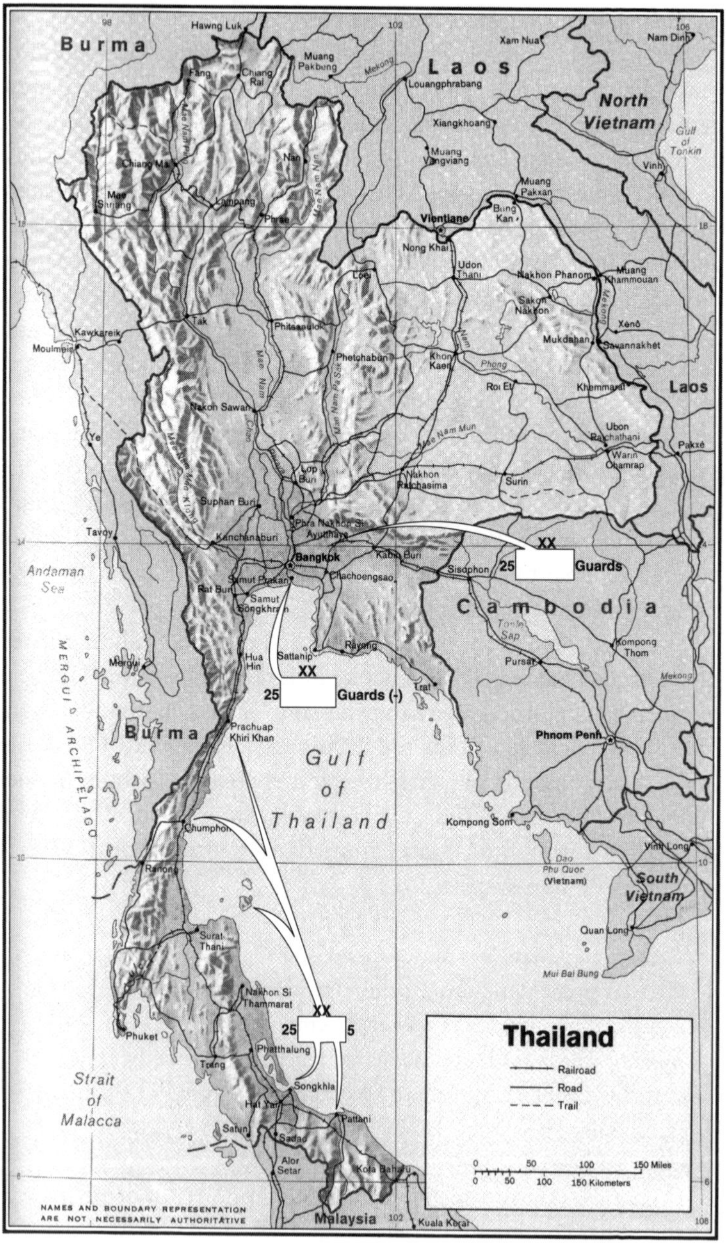

All that has so far emerged regarding the Thai attitude to the "New Order" has been the treacherous action of the dictator Luang Phibunsongkhram and his advisors in handing the country over to the Japanese, while but a moment before they had been professing their intentions of defending Thailand's neutrality.[18]

Wendell Blanchard observed that "Premier Phibunsongkhram did his best to help the Japanese as little as possible while seeming to aid them."[19] Retired Air Chief Marshal Thawi Chunlasap, a major force in the resistance movement and a powerful figure in modern Thailand, declared in his memoirs that Phibun had followed the right policy. Thawi believes that by allowing Japanese troops to enter Thailand, the premier spared Thailand the destruction that Thawi witnessed in Malaya, and that the world realized that Thailand was too small to successfully oppose Japan by force.[20]

THE THAI CAPITULATION TO JAPANESE DEMANDS

The agreement reached between Japan and Thailand on 9 December 1941 was a short but masterful expression of immediate capitulation by Thailand to the reality of Japanese military invasion, coupled with face-saving gestures designed to appease Thai national pride. Thawi Bunyaket has summarized the four main provisions of the agreement:[21]

1. The Thai government permitted Japan to send troops through Thailand to other countries in the region, notably Malaya and Burma.
2. The Japanese troops would not disarm Thai forces.
3. Japanese forces would only pass through, not remain in, Bangkok.
4. The agreement was only military in nature and did not imply a political or military alliance. No further requirements were to be levied on Thailand.

This agreement accomplished several purposes. For the first time,

Thailand signed a military agreement with Japan. At the same time, the Thai government placed several limitations on the extent of the agreement. Thailand protected its sovereignty by using the word "permit" *(anuyat)* concerning Japanese military activities inside Thailand. While written to be as inoffensive as possible, the agreement was a precursor of future demands. The Thai Cabinet felt that it had no choice but to appease the Japanese forces inside their country. Thawi Bunyaket felt certain that the United States and England would understand the circumstances leading to the alliance with Japan.[22]

Initially the Japanese undertook to make the Thai position as comfortable as possible. Troop units that conducted the initial invasion of Thailand were moved out of the country as promptly as transportation facilities allowed. Guards Division, Twenty-fifth Army, which had "captured" Bangkok, moved by land to Malaya on 21 December, as did most of the Fifth Division.[23]

The agreement of 9 December 1941 was in part a compromise, for the Japanese actually had presented the Thai government with a choice of four courses of action. The four choices presented Thailand with varying levels of security and guaranteed sovereignty. A measure of "sweetening" was added, by which Japan would return to Thai jurisdiction certain territory lost to England in the colonies of Burma and Malaya. These so-called "lost lands" included much of the Burmese province of Keng Tung bordering Thailand on the north and the northwest, and the four northernmost Malayan states (Kelantan, Kedah, Perlis, and Trengganu).

The first option presented to Thailand called for complete cooperation between Thailand and Japan on political, military, and economic matters. In return for these concessions Japan guaranteed Thailand's sovereignty and the return to Thailand of the "lost lands." The Thai government rejected the option as being politically too binding. The second choice called for Thailand to enter the Axis as a full partner with Japan, Germany, and Italy. Japan offered the same concessions to Thailand as in the first option but the Thai government also rejected this second choice. A third choice was for Thailand and Japan to sign a defense pact without involving the Axis partners. This was also rejected by the Thai government.

The fourth choice offered by Japan called for the two countries to sign a mutual defense pact of limited coverage. The pact allowed passage of Japanese forces through Thailand but did not commit Thailand to the Axis or to full-scale operations in support of the Japanese war effort in Southeast Asia. This choice placed the lowest level of commitment on Thailand but also offered the lowest amount of security for it did not guarantee Thailand's sovereignty. No mention was made of the return of any territories in Burma and Malaya. While the benefits were the smallest of the four options available, this course of action also placed the least degree of obligation on the Thai government. This is why Phibun chose the fourth option.[24]

THE JAPANESE-THAILAND TREATY OF ALLIANCE AND THE THAI DECLARATION OF WAR

A review of the literature indicates that the Thai government was generally resigned to the fact that the agreement of 9 December would not satisfy the Japanese. On 21 December, after continued political and military pressure, Thailand and Japan signed a "Treaty of Alliance" with heavy emphasis on military and economic cooperation in the event of war. The treaty had five major provisions.

First, Thailand and Japan espoused mutual respect for the independence and sovereignty of the other. Second, both signatories were obligated to render assistance to its ally if either became engaged in a conflict with a third country. Third, the two countries would determine the details of providing such assistance through mutual agreement. Fourth, neither signatory could engage in a separate peace without the consent of the other. Finally, the treaty was effective for a period of ten years.[25]

Once that treaty was signed it was only a matter of time before Thailand was forced to declare war against the United States and England. A combination of the military presence of the Japanese troops in Thailand and the consequences of a failure to abide by Japanese desires forced the Thai government to act. Luang Wichit

Wathakan, who had replaced Direk Chaiyanam as foreign minister in mid December 1941, observed that within the Japanese forces themselves there was a dispute over whether or not Thailand should be forced to declare war against the Allies. The Japanese government urged such a step by Thailand to show political support by an Asian partner. However, the Japanese army attempted to delay a declaration of war until they could complete the evacuation to Japan of American and British economic assets.[26]

Phibun moved to consolidate his power in the weeks following the Japanese invasion of Thailand. He removed Pridi and Direk from the Cabinet by sending Direk to Japan as ambassador and giving Pridi a ceremonial position as a member of the Regency Council that represented King Ananda Mahidol while he was attending school in Switzerland. Other Pridi supporters also were forced out of the government but those in lower positions generally remained in their offices throughout the war. Pridi came to rely extensively on their support.

Wichit Wathakan supported on several grounds those who wanted to declare war against the Allies. Their reasons included the diplomatic and international obligations incurred by the 21 December treaty with Japan; the chance to avoid the embarrassment of having Thai forces disarmed by the Japanese; the opportunity to intern American and British subjects in Thailand rather than leaving them to the Japanese; and the ability to assume control of Allied assets in Thailand for the duration of the war without having them removed to Japan.[27]

Thailand finally declared war on the United States and England on 25 January 1942. Phibun found this task physically difficult and the actual signing of the declaration of war was illegal. Thai law required that all members of the Council of Regents had to sign laws and declarations issued in the name of the king. But Pridi, the newest member of the council, went into hiding to avoid signing the declaration of war. The document was returned to Phibun with only two of the required three signatures. Phibun ordered Pridi's name to be added to the document.[28] This series of maneuvers would assume great significance in the political aftermath of the war. It gave Pridi and other Thai officials the much needed technicality to void the declaration when, at the end of the war, Thailand began its political struggle to achieve legitimacy. Pridi's forged signature became a major point of evidence cited at the end of the war to substantiate the claim that the Thai declaration of war was illegal and therefore did not reflect the will of the Thai people.

One of the main arguments concerning the declaration of war was whether or not it was a genuine expression of the Thai government and people, or a unilateral decision by Phibun. Most accounts of the time indicate that the entire Cabinet was not consulted in the decision. The fact that not all three members of the Council of Regents signed the pact has been mentioned. But the fact remains that the prime minister of Thailand took the action as leader of the government, whatever the degree of unanimity within the government might have been. It was therefore an expression of the will of the government, even if it was improperly drawn. A leading postwar Thai historian has written:

> The declaration of war was a strange affair because Parliament was not consulted and Mr. Pridi . . . went into hiding in order to escape the counter signing of the declaration. The declaration was therefore highly irregular and was never accepted by the Americans as constitutional, legal, nor representing the actual will of the people. [29]

CONCLUSION

Thailand entered World War II amid tremendous military and political pressures applied by Japan. The country's strategic location in Southeast Asia was vital to the Japanese war effort in Malaya, Burma, and India. By exploiting Thailand's nationalism and strong feelings of sovereignty Japan gained an important beachhead from which to launch military operations without having to occupy Thailand. At the same time Japan maneuvered Thailand into an overt partnership. Thailand's "voluntary" alliance with Japan served as an effective means to demonstrate solidarity in Asia and lent credence to Japan's claims of a voluntary growth of its Greater East Asia Co-prosperity Sphere.

Thailand's internal political situation lent itself to formation of a resistance movement. The country's political elite was split into a military faction led by Phibun and a smaller civilian elite headed by Pridi. The long history of conflict between the two men and their supporters made it perhaps inevitable that Pridi would form a resistance organization against Phibun and the Japanese occupation forces. He had the advantage of personal power, a small group of loyal followers, and many years of experience in political opposition to the Phibun government. The Japanese demand for a declaration of war by Thailand against the Western democracies provided a natural focus of outrage around which the Thai people could rally regardless of their domestic political sympathies.

The significance of the illegally drawn document that was the formal instrument of Thailand's declaration of war became increasingly important as the war progressed and the resistance movement expanded. As will be seen, the resistance leaders directed their efforts toward discrediting Phibun's basic position that placed Thailand in the Axis camp instead of on the side of the Allies. Finally, the illegality of the manner in which Thailand entered the war on the side of Japan became an important diplomatic symbol for the resistance movement and its worldwide supporters.

CHAPTER TWO

FORMATION OF THE THAI RESISTANCE MOVEMENT

The following description of Thai nationalism suggests it provided a congenial base for the formation of a resistance movement:

> The Thai love their country. They are aware that it has been the 'Land of the Thai' for many centuries, and they are proud that only rarely and briefly has it been under foreign rule. They have a very fully developed sense of nationality, an amalgam of ideas of sharing a common land, a common language, and a common religion—all under one king. While fully developed, this nationalism is not aggressive or exclusive. It is the quiet and confident attitude of a people who value their way of life but who have no wish to impose it on others.[1]

The Japanese occupation of Thailand was an accomplished fact before the end of 1941. The occupation was not physically harsh as in eastern China and the Philippines, for the facade of partnership required the Japanese to moderate their presence. But if not harsh it was no less onerous to the Thai. The occupation was an infringement on Thai sovereignty regardless of diplomatic agreements that cloaked the presence of Japanese forces in legitimacy. After World War II, General Net Khemayothin, a major figure in the Thai underground, paid tribute to the involvement of the entire Thai population when he told Direk:

[In addition] to everyone who cooperated . . . there were also 17 million people who believed in freedom in the resistance. They did what they could to strengthen patriotism and force the Japanese to leave Thailand as fast as possible.[2]

The Thai peoples' strong nationalism and faith in their independence fostered resistance movements simultaneously in Thailand, the United States, and in England. Available literature suggests that the movements arose spontaneously. After a small leadership core began to direct activity the movements began to establish contact and coordination with each other. The ability of the Thai resistance effort to establish these important avenues of communication was of major significance in the establishment of a viable worldwide resistance effort.

BEGINNINGS OF RESISTANCE IN THAILAND

Thai Foreign Minister Direk Chaiyanam told a member of the British diplomatic mission in Bangkok on 6 December 1941, that " . . . if the Japanese do invade us, I know that people like Nai Pridi and myself will never accept the situation. You may be sure we will work against them."[3]

Organized resistance to the Japanese began before the 9 December agreement was signed. One source reported with some melodrama, "On that infamous December 8, 1941, while the average citizen of Thailand stood dazed and weeping in the streets watching Japanese trucks roll by . . . . on that very day the first attempt to organize systematic resistance was made."[4]

The first serious and purposeful meeting of anti-Japanese Thai leaders took place on 11 December 1941. This meeting, composed of leading civilian members of the government and influential elders from the Thai autocracy, was an informal gathering which reinforced the participants' opposition to Phibun's policies as well as a newly discovered anti-Japanese patriotism. Those in attendance included a cross-section of Thai civilian leadership who were eventually to form the core of the Thai resistance movement during the war. This group used the code name "X.O. Group" to designate the inner circle of leadership within the resistance movement regardless of membership at any one time.[5] Many Thais at this first meeting had been part of Pridi's civilian faction of the 1932 coup d'etat and turned again to his leadership.

Pridi Banomyong resumed the mantle of leadership he held during the 1932 coup d'etat. An economist whose views were considered too radical by many people, Pridi had been forced to deny on several occasions that he was a communist. Regardless of his left-of-center economic and political leanings, Pridi had a large following in Thailand. He used the prestige of his position on the Council of Regents to advantage, and enlarged the personal stature of what had been a largely ceremonial position. Pridi was the leader of the resistance movement from the beginning, a position he filled by force of leadership and the respect engendered by his prior performance. Pridi called the initial meeting of the X.O. Group at his home on Silom Road. Throughout the war, similar gatherings would be held at both Pridi's home and at his official Regency residence.[6]

Direk Chaiyanam, who had been foreign minister on 9 December 1941, was removed by Phibun and sent to Tokyo as ambassador to Japan. He returned from Japan in 1943 and held several other positions in government.[7] Rear Admiral Sangwon Yuthakit, deputy commander of the Royal Thai Navy, the highest ranking military member of the X.O. Group, also commanded all military police in Bangkok. Sa-nguan Tularak was a member of the National Assembly and chairman of the Tobacco Monopoly in the Ministry of Finance. Four other members of the National Assembly and long-time Pridi confidantes at the meeting were Luang Kri Dechatiwong, Charun Sunsaeng, Thongplao Chonaphum, and Thawi Tawetikun.

Pridi and his supporters gave almost immediate consideration to establishment of a government-in-exile. They foresaw the capitulation to Japan as the first event in Thailand's progress toward formal alliance with Japan. Pridi had spent years opposing Phibun's military dictatorship, so Phibun's increased strength as war approached caused a reaction from Pridi. However, Pridi postponed plans for forming a government-in-exile because of the tremendous difficulties involved but did not discard the idea until late in the war.

At least part of Pridi's concern for the possibility of forming a government-in-exile may have stemmed from a fear that he would be detained by Phibun because of their political differences. Since Pridi's concern on this issue arose before Thailand formally entered the war, the domestic consideration is significant. Pridi's initial worry was not that he would be arrested by Japanese authorities, but that Phibun would remove him from effective leadership for domestic political reasons. Apparently Phibun never seriously considered such a step and in a short time the more pressing issues of active anti-Japanese resistance overshadowed the two leaders' domestic differences.

One of the first plans discussed was to establish a government opposed to Japan in Nakhon Sawan province in the north. Such a plan depended on military support from Thai army units in the region as well as from military forces stationed in Chiang Mai and Phitsanulok farther north. Such an opposition government, once established and secure, some argued, would appeal to the Thai to support it rather than Phibun and the Japanese. But this plan, idealistically appealing, was also discarded as being too large in scope and too difficult to implement.

The X.O. Group adopted the remaining alternative, the formation of an active resistance movement that would gradually draw military and political strength from sources both inside and outside Thailand.[8] This decision, made before the end of 1941, was the basis for the future resistance movement in Thailand. One resistance leader, Mom Chao (M.C.) Karawik Chakraphan, has pointed out that:

> The underground movement was born the very moment the cease-fire was ordered by the government of Luang Phibul. Owing to the overwhelming superiority of the Japanese Army in men, materials and technique at that moment, this movement could indulge in nothing but passive resistance. This movement was considerable, but little could it do until enemy surveillance should slacken and modern materials be forthcoming.[9]

There was little doubt that Phibun knew his policy of cooperation with Japan would be resisted by many. Within a week of the capitulation a group of unnamed men plotted to steal a train in Bangkok to travel to northern Thailand. They planned to dynamite the tunnel on the Lampang–Chiang Mai border to prevent pursuit and then actively to oppose the Phibun government. The plan was betrayed to Phibun who seized the train before it was boarded.[10] Whether that particular incident was a part of Pridi's initial planning cannot be determined with certainty because the names of those involved were never revealed. Yet the coincidence is striking.

Another anti-Phibun resistance group was formed by Chamkat Phalangkun, who was to play a major role in consolidating the worldwide Thai resistance movement. Chamkat's group, called Ku Chat (Liberation), merged with Pridi's as soon as Chamkat became aware of Pridi's position in the fledgling resistance movement. Chamkat, who had worked with Pridi in the 1932 coup d'etat, believed that Pridi was the best qualified person to lead the overall resistance movement. Other members of the Ku Chat group were Thawin Udon, Chamlong Daorueang, Komet Khrueatrachu and Yon Somanon.[11] All joined with Pridi and later filled positions of importance in the resistance leadership. Chamkat became the first man to establish contact with the Allies in China. Thawin later commanded all underground guerrilla activities in northeast Thailand and also traveled to China. Their roles in the resistance movement are discussed in more detail in later chapters.

Other resistance groups joined Pridi as word spread that a resistance movement was being formed. Pridi and others in leadership positions recruited those whom they knew and trusted. The formal Thai infrastructure, police, military services, and the civil service, supplied an extensive pool of people for the resistance movement. Malai Chuphanit, author of the definitive work on the leadership of the Thai resistance movement, stated that most government officials felt it was their duty to join the resistance to uphold the honor of the country.[12]

This statement by Malai is supported by Western observers' reports. One author reported, "The vast majority of . . . Thai still cherish the hope of democracy . . . . The Thai always valued freedom

. . . it would not be too much to expect considerable guerrilla help on the part of the peasants, and the defection of the Thai Army."[13]

Margaret Landon reinforced this point of view with another observation concerning the Thai people's spontaneous joining of the resistance movement:

> Long after Japanese control of their country was an accomplished fact, Thai . . . were still coming to provincial centers to volunteer for the fight they took for granted was being made against the enemy. The Thai underground . . . was born less than twelve hours after the Japanese armies occupied Bangkok. Initial resistance was unplanned, sporadic, ineffective, but it revealed the sense of futile anger that stirred the Thai people.[14]

In the United States, Thai minister M.R. Seni Pramoj observed, "While it would be too optimistic to speak at this juncture of the growth of a spirit of open revolt, I am satisfied that there are signs of dissention and that these signs, though mere seeds, may ultimately blossom into an organized opposition to the invaders."[15]

Pridi established four initial goals for underground activities. They included taking steps to reduce the power and influence of Phibun's government and its policies with Japan; conducting sabotage operations against the Japanese army; spreading rumors through propaganda of distrust and dissention between Phibun and the Japanese; and finally, and the most urgent, establishing contact with the Allies.[16]

The greatest initial obstacles encountered by the resistance movement were problems and difficulties of external communications. Efforts to gain communications with the Allies and with sympathetic Thais in other countries were repeatedly stymied, resulting in much frustration and heartbreak. Although Pridi was uncertain, he believed that overseas Thais had also started resistance movements in the United States and England. It was essential to Thailand's future independence that a united resistance effort be formed as soon as possible so it could be used as an effective political bargaining tool at the end of the war. He hoped that England and the United States had recognized the difficulties that forced Thailand to declare war. Pridi believed the Allies would ignore the declaration and give continued support to Thai independence after the war. Through perseverance, patience, and luck, external contacts were eventually established that resulted in a worldwide Thai resistance movement.

The resistance effort in Thailand began in December 1941, centered around Pridi Banomyong and a small group of his loyal supporters. The core of the resistance leadership, composed largely of civilians dedicated to democracy and opposed politically to both the Phibun philosophy and the Japanese occupation, shared many qualities. They had been associated with Pridi since the 1932 coup d'etat and shared his liberal views and political beliefs. They were experienced in underground activity as a result of their participation in planning the 1932 coup d'etat. Although most of them had politically opposed Phibun for years, this was not their sole reason for joining a resistance movement. They were patriotic citizens who hoped to maintain Thailand's independence after the war and, at the same time, to lead the country back to the democratic tradition they had attempted to establish in 1932.

Most members of the initial X.O. Group were civilians. The few military members were navy officers; there were no army or police officers in the initial circle of leadership. Many of the eventual leaders of the resistance came from the army and police but they did not join with Pridi's group until 1943 or later. While this closely knit group struggled to organize an anti-Japanese resistance organization in Thailand that was composed of all elements of society, Thai students and expatriates in the United States and England attempted to form their relatively small Thai communities into anti-Japanese resistance centers as well.

BEGINNINGS OF THE RESISTANCE MOVEMENT IN THE UNITED STATES

The relationship between Thailand and the United States during World War II was unusual, due in large part to the foresight of some American leaders as well as the astute actions of the Thai

21

minister, M.R. Seni Pramoj. The long history of friendship between the two countries also contributed to this relationship. King Mongkut's offer of war elephants to President Lincoln during the American Civil War is often cited as a symbol of a unique and long-lasting international friendship between the two countries. But in 1942 the ramifications of a declaration of war by Thailand against the United States had to be considered.

The United States did not reciprocate Thailand's declaration of war. Diplomats and historians gave several reasons for American forbearance, but one of the most dramatic causes of the continued American friendship for Thailand was the action of the Thai minister in Washington. On the same day that the Phibun government declared war on the United States and England, M.R. Seni publicly announced that the true sympathies of the Thai were with the Allies, not Phibun.[17] He declared that the Thai Legation in Washington, D.C. was independent of the government in Bangkok. When M.R. Seni arrived at the U.S. State Department for a meeting with Secretary of State Cordell Hull, apparently to deliver a copy of the Thai declaration of war, ". . . [he] tapped his coat and said to Hull: 'I'm keeping the declaration in my pocket because I am convinced it does not represent the will of the Thai people. With American help, I propose to prove it.'"[18] Thailand's declaration of war against the United States was never given to Secretary Hull.

M.R. Seni, speaking to students after the war, recounted his feelings at that time:

> During the War, the United States proved to be our best friend, helping us when we had fallen to the worst, at which time we could not foresee a dim light of independence. The relationship between Thailand and the United States of America during these days was tied up so tightly that it can hardly be broken off . . . Thai history showed me that if we . . . waved our Thai National Flag from the top of the pole in the Thai Embassy compound, then all Thai people would join us to drive the Japanese away . . . our Embassy . . . decided not to observe the Thai government's surrender to the Japanese . . . and to . . . organize resistance against the Japanese, believing that all Thai would help one another to regain Independence from the Japanese.[19]

M.R. Seni's pro-Western stance contributed significantly to the favorable American policy toward Thailand during the war. Other embassy staffers who assisted him in forming an active resistance movement in the United States were Luang Dithakan Phakdi, first secretary, and Colonel M.L. Khap Kunchon, the military attache. Thai students volunteered to join any unit that would fight the Japanese. As time progressed they were assigned to a variety of American governmental agencies such as the Office of War Information, the War Department, and the Office of Strategic Services (OSS).[20]

M.R. Seni formulated three steps in his policy to maintain the independence, sovereignty, and self-respect of the Thai people. First, he made known the fact that the Thai minister had refused to deliver the Thai declaration of war to the American secretary of state. Second, he called on Thai citizens in the United States to volunteer to join either American military forces or an American-sanctioned Thai military organization. Third, he attempted to influence all Thais living abroad to oppose the Japanese occupation of Thailand.[21] He made it clear in numerous public interviews and written statements that the Thai government in Bangkok was a puppet of the Japanese and did not represent the wishes of the Thai people.

M.R. Seni appealed for and received assistance from the United States government. He made three principal requests to Washington: first, assistance in funding and training Thais living in the U.S. to return to Thailand to oppose the Japanese by force; second, assistance in communicating with Thailand; third, permission to carry on secret, unpublicized diplomatic activities with other countries for the support of Thailand. The United States, alone among the Allies in sympathizing with M.R. Seni, approved all three of these requests for support to the new resistance movement.

M.R. Seni called his organization the Seri Thai (Free Thai) and launched it with a manifesto of purpose and goals.[22] The manifesto declared that, *inter alia:*

1) The Seri Thai was not a political party but an organization whose main objective was to restore Thailand's Independence.

2) The Japanese army was the enemy of the Thai because their armed forces had invaded Thailand.

3) The Bangkok government was a puppet government because it had cooperated with the enemy against the will of the people.

4) The Seri Thai regarded itself as the representative agency representing the will of the Thai people everywhere.

5) The Seri Thai would not interfere with the law of succession of the king.

6) A constitutional government and democracy would be restored to Thailand after the country's freedom was restored. The Seri Thai would release all political prisoners and would organize a Peoples' Court to investigate those who had cooperated with the enemy.

American support for and training of members of the Thai resistance force began in April 1942, under the aegis of the OSS. This action required a major policy decision at the highest level of government, since Thais in the United States would have been subject to a draft into regular military units. Approval for the formation of a special unit of Thai members was a unique and important step in the continued viability of a worldwide resistance movement.

Student leaders in the U.S. drew up a plan of operations and presented it to the OSS in May. As events turned out, many of its initial proposals were carried out as Thai agents were trained and infiltrated Thailand during the ensuing three years. Among other things it called for the Thai student volunteers to work in pairs during infiltration, suggested the launch base be located in southern China, called for an emphasis on intelligence gathering and communciations with the Allied forces, and called for unity of effort among external and internal Thai resistance elements.[23]

Eventually dozens of Thai volunteers in the United States completed a vigorous training program to prepare them for guerrilla operations and intelligence missions in Thailand. The training program was under the direction of Colonel Preston Goodfellow (OSS) and Dr. Kenneth Landon.[24] Dr. Landon, who had spent many years in Thailand, was indispensable in planning, organizing, and providing operational assistance to the program. The American branch of the Thai resistance movement evolved from an unusual blend of Thai leadership. M.R. Seni was appointed to his ministerial position by Phibun, although Seni's political views were more attuned to those of Pridi. Colonel Khap was generally believed to have been sent specifically to the United States by Phibun to keep a wary eye on M.R. Seni and to report on the minister's activities. Although of different political persuasions, the two men forged an excellent partnership in leadership of the American branch of the Seri Thai.

THE BEGINNING OF THE THAI RESISTANCE MOVEMENT IN ENGLAND

Thai resistance efforts in England were not as easily organized as those in the United States. When Thailand declared war, England reciprocated by immediately declaring war on Thailand. Throughout the war, and at its conclusion, the British government considered Thailand to be an enemy state. M.R. Seni observed that the Thai ambassador in London would have been wiser to have refused to deliver the declaration of war and to have disassociated his embassy from the Thai government in Bangkok.[25]

The Thai resistance movement enjoyed strong support from Thais living in England since many of the students had been anti-Phibun before the war. The added incentive of patriotism and anti-Japanese feelings strengthened support for an organized resistance movement. Nominal Phibun sympathizers joined the movement to assist in expelling the Japanese from Thailand.[26] While not initially enjoying support from the British government, and without the prestige that resistance efforts had received in the United States, Thai citizens in England succeeded in forming an active resistance organization. They repudiated the declaration of war against England and publicly supported the Allies' efforts against Japan.

The resistance effort in England suffered, in its early stages, from both the lack of a strong leader, geographic isolation from resistance leaders in the United States, and factionalism. Accounts of the period list several persons as "chief" of the Thai resistance effort in England. As a result, organization proceeded more slowly than in the United States. Yet the Thais in England had the advantage of knowing that a formal resistance movement had been established in Washington, D.C. A small cadre of leaders emerged from the Thai community in London to create the nucleus of the resistance. Credit for this first effort at organization was given by Puay Ungphakon to Sano Tanbunyuen, who was assisted by Sano Ninkhamhaeng and Sawang Samkoset.

Sano Tanbunyuen communicated with M.R. Seni in Washington in April 1942, requesting that Seni visit England to assist in organizing the local resistance movement. Sano also hoped that Seni would be able to influence the British government to take a more sympathetic attitude toward Thailand. Although Seni realized that there was potential for an organized resistance effort in England, he was too heavily committed in the United States to travel to London. He sent as his representative Mani Sanasen, an employee of the League of Nations in Switzerland. Mani, the son of the Thai ambassador to England, began his role as the unofficial leader of the resistance movement in England during the spring of 1942. He served primarily as a high-level link between the Thais in England and the Thais in the United States. Mani confirmed Sano Tanbunyuen as leader of the movement in England and appointed Puay Ungphakon as an additional contact for the local Thai. Mani also devoted much of his effort toward gaining permission for Thai students to join the British army.[27] Sano's strengthened position provided a common bond for the Thai community. He and Mani directed the Thai efforts in England without opposition until the war ended.

British intelligence was keenly interested in exploiting the Thai community's desire to serve the war effort. Special Operations Executive (SOE), counterpart to the intelligence collection arm of OSS, designated M.C. Suphasawatwongsanit Sawatdiwat (known in most accounts as Prince Subha or Subhasavasti) as their own "chief" of the Thai student movement.[28] SOE gave him the code name "Major Arun."[29]

Although Major Arun was designated as leader of organized resistance activity by SOE, his personality and royalist beliefs made him unpopular with the Thai students.[30] He had been exiled from Thailand after the 1932 coup d'etat because of his extreme royalist sympathies. For these reasons he was politically unacceptable to liberal students and post-1932 Thai leaders. However, he later acquitted himself admirably as a member of the resistance element infiltrated into Thailand and also held important high-level liaison posts.

Major Arun was assigned to lead the paramilitary element of the Thai resistance effort in England. Sir Andrew Gilchrist, then a member of the British Foreign Office who worked with Thai operations in SOE during much of the war, was impressed by Major Arun.

Arun was the only Siamese the British recognized as being "good," presumably because he was politically unacceptable to nearly all his countrymen . . . . It was inevitable that Arun's obvious political unsuitability should later lead to friction and suspicion. But Arun was a wholehearted Siamese patriot, a brave man who was willing to risk his life . . . for Siam.[31]

Despite a somewhat shaky beginning, the British arm of the resistance movement was to perform effectively in the overall war effort. Major Arun acted as chief of the paramilitary element that was to become engaged in anti-Japanese operations in Southeast Asia. Mani acted as M.R. Seni's political representative in England, while Sano Tanbunyuen coordinated the Thai community's resistance efforts inside England. The triumvirate of leadership worked well together and was able to direct operations in England with efficiency and in close coordination with M.R. Seni in the United States.

POLITICAL INTEGRATION OF THE SERI THAI

By early 1942 Thai resistance movements were established in the United States, Thailand, and England. M.R. Seni assumed control of the Thai in the United States and England, who were known as the "Outside Group" (Phai Nok Prathet). The movement had the advantages of efficient communication and ease of travel between countries and was able to operate in close coordination in political matters.

While the Thais were closely cooperative, their Western sponsors (OSS and SOE) lacked such cohesion until the final stages of the war. While nominally moving toward a common goal, OSS and SOE competed throughout the war for a series of "firsts" to enhance organizational prestige and foster the interests of their respective governments. The two agencies, instead of conducting joint planning and operations from the start, operated with little contact with each other until the final year of the war. The competitive nature of their respective operations concerning Thailand served only to isolate the Thais from each other and prolonged the effort to install Thai agents in Thailand.

The United States and England approached Thailand from significantly different policy positions. The United States considered Thailand a friendly country occupied by Japan, while England regarded Thailand as an enemy country actively cooperating with Japan. They were unable to decide until after the war what course to take with respect to Thailand's continued sovereignty and independence. This difference in attitude toward Thailand contributed to their mutual reluctance to operate fully in supporting the Thai resistance movement. This also led to uncoordinated intelligence operations in Southeast Asia, which slowed collection of important intelligence information in the region. These differences were to play a major role in determining the external political atmosphere with which the Seri Thai leaders had to be concerned.

M.R. Seni was aware of the nature of the political problem he faced in insuring the continued viability of his country after the war. It is probable that Pridi had some knowledge of the differing policies of England and the United States as well. It was not until the resistance leadership monitored radio broadcasts from the United States that they learned America had refrained from declaring war on Thailand, while England had done so. Pridi also knew that Thailand faced major political difficulties. The resistance leadership probably realized from the start that their tasks encompassed both paramilitary missions normally associated with underground resistance operations as well as a massive political rehabilitation program to convince the Allies that Thailand was in fact sympathetic to the Allies and not to Japan. These political realities were to take first priority in virtually every plan and activity of the Thai resistance movement.

SUMMARY

Resistance movements established in Thailand, England, and the United States began plans for anti-Japanese activities shortly after Thailand was invaded by the Japanese. Pridi Banomyong's efforts in Thailand started slowly, centered on a small group of loyal supporters called the X.O. Group. His earliest efforts were devoted to forming a small cadre of leadership and to establishing contact with Thai communities abroad. Both the Thailand and the Western elements of the resistance gained membership from patriotic Thais anxious to expel the Japanese from Thailand and to maintain Thai independence and sovereignty. Most of the initial leaders of the resistance movement were liberal-minded civilians, experienced through participation in the 1932 coup d'etat, and opposed to the policies and philosophy of Marshal Phibun.

The focus of activity outside Thailand was in Washington, D.C. where Thailand's minister assumed control of Seri Thai elements in the United States and England. M.R. Seni successfully obtained the support of the American government for his movement and began coordinated efforts to establish a paramilitary force to actively oppose the Japanese.

Movements inside Thailand (Phai Nai Prathet) and abroad (Phai Nok Prathet) formed simultaneously for the same purposes, and were composed of leaders dedicated to Thailand's independence and of a political persuasion generally opposed to Phibun's dictatorship. Yet contact between Bangkok and resistance centers abroad was virtually nonexistent until 1943. Pridi had no assurance that active Thai resistance organizations had been formed in the West, although through monitored radio broadcasts he had received strong indications that such organizations had been formed. The Allies were generally ignorant of conditions inside Thailand. They did not know of the nature of Pridi's resistance movement until 1944. Thai resistance leaders in the United States and England had no indisputable knowledge that resistance operations had been started inside Thailand. Most important, the Allies had an immediate requirement for information on the political and military situation inside Thailand. This need for intelligence was the primary reason why Allied intelligence agencies made the decisions necessary to actively support the Thai resistance effort. The most pressing need during the formative period in the resistance effort was, therefore, to establish a communications link between Thailand and the Allies. Only after such contact had been made could the Allies determine the degree of resistance inside Thailand and begin their active support of the Seri Thai.

THE RESISTANCE GROUPS STRUGGLE TO ACHIEVE CONTACT, 1942–1943

COMMUNICATIONS EFFORTS FROM THE UNITED STATES

M.R. Seni's appeal for assistance on behalf of the Thai resistance movement was well received in the United States. The political decision to recognize the Thai Legation and Minister Seni as the representatives of the Thai people enabled the United States to assist the movement without violating international law. Efforts to form a link between the resistance leadership in Washington and the underground believed to exist in Bangkok began early in 1942.

The Office of War Information (OWI) responded almost immediately to M.R. Seni's request for broadcast assistance. Several Thai students went to work for the agency. Initially they provided background information on Thailand, translated programs into Thai, and prepared their own programs for broadcast to Thailand. Later they also became broadcasters. Radio station KGIA (San Francisco), owned by the government, became the primary outlet for the broadcast of native language programs to the occupied countries in the Pacific, including Thailand. This station aired the first information to Thailand that the United States had not declared war on the country. Similar transmitters were located under British control in India, Australia, and Chungking, China.

The Seri Thai appeal for Thai students to join either the American armed forces or an independent military organization was not considered practical by the War Department. However, Thai students worked for the department and provided needed information for empty military intelligence files on that part of the world. Since the greatest potential for a Thai paramilitary force was in the field of intelligence, the OSS was the logical agency to organize the Thai volunteers. OSS viewed the potential of a Thai unit from an intelligence standpoint rather than as a political asset. Usable information on Southeast Asia was scarce in the American intelligence community, which had historically been oriented toward Europe. Thailand was "the biggest information blind spot in the entire Far East."[1] The OSS needed information to support Allied operations in Burma, to locate feasible tactical and strategic bombing targets, to monitor activity at prisoner-of-war camps in Southeast Asia, and to assess the strength of Japanese forces throughout this region.

M.R. Seni was primarily interested in the long-range political benefits that would accrue to Thailand as a result of resistance activities. He was apprehensive that the Thai declaration of war would pose grave consequences for his nation at the end of the war. Seni had no doubt that the Allies would win the war and feared that England would demand special rights in Thailand. At best he suspected the British would seize control of the Thai economy, at worst that Thailand would become another British colonial possession. This fate was a distinct possibility because Thailand lay between British colonies in Burma and Malaya and was adjacent to French Indochina.

M.R. Seni considered as his main responsibility the creation of a favorable image of Thailand in the United States and England, and he believed that the participation of the Thai community in the war effort would further this image. The United States' favorable response to his forceful rejection of the Thai government in Bangkok led to his concentration of resistance efforts in America. He encouraged Thai citizens to enter any needed activity, whether broadcasting, military service, or intelligence operations. When it became obvious that America's greatest requirement was intelligence, and the formation of a group of volunteers for intelligence-gathering operations, M.R. Seni enthusiastically supported the project.

OSS had no knowledge of the situation inside Thailand. There were indications that the Thai people had not welcomed the Japanese occupation. But there was no information available on the strength of an internal resistance movement, if such a movement existed. The Chinese provided some information from their extensive intelligence network in Southeast Asia, but they made available only a limited amount of the information obtained by their intelligence headquarters in southern China.[2] OSS began planning to infiltrate intelligence agents into Thailand without any reliable intelligence on the internal situation in the country. In intelligence parlance, it was to be a "blind operation."

When word circulated in early 1942 that a limited number of Thai would be trained to return to Thailand as intelligence agents, several dozen responded. They completed a strenuous program of training in such subjects as guerrilla operations, intelligence collection, and physical conditioning. Originally the group was called the Free Thai Army. Each trainee held a military rank. Most became second lieutenants in the Free Thai Army. However, several of the students were already members of the Thai armed forces, studying in the U.S. on military scholarships. Those men were promoted to ranks ranging from second lieutenant to captain.[3] The first group of trainees completed training in January 1943.

At that stage of operations a remarkable OSS officer, Nicol Smith, joined the OSS program to fill the roles of quartermaster, paymaster, commander, and father-confessor to the Thai agents. His account of subsequent experiences with the Thai operation (cited herein) is the most detailed narrative in print in English of this aspect of OSS operations during World War II.

The first group of twenty-one Thai agents left the United States by ship in March 1943.[4] Nicol Smith accompanied them on the voyage, while Colonel Khap Kunchon flew ahead to Chungking as M.R. Seni's representative and nominal commander of the Thai agents. (A roster of these agents is given in the appendices.) The group sailed through the Panama Canal and south around Australia and on to Bombay. They moved via Calcutta to an OSS camp in northeast India for final training and conditioning. They finally arrived at OSS headquarters outside Chungking in the early summer of 1943. M.L. Khap rejoined the group there.[5]

Almost immediately, the American-sponsored team encountered the high-level political intrigue that was to handicap Allied intelligence operations in Southeast Asia. The American intelligence apparatus in Asia was an organization with headquarters in both Kandy and Calcutta and subsections in many other locations involved in directing operations. This arrangement not surprisingly resulted in confusion in the direction of intelligence missions. Furthermore, the presence of other Allied intelligence agencies in the area, responsive to their own headquarters and often operating independently of each other, compounded the confusion. Even well-meaning attempts at cooperation and coordination failed in the welter of conflicting interests at work in the region.

Control of early American intelligence operations in Southeast Asia was diffused. The authority for OSS to conduct operations into Thailand was contained in Joint Chiefs of Staff Directive 245 (subsequently referred to as JCS 245). It specified that intelligence operations were to be conducted under the control of the Sino-American Cooperative Organization (SACO), composed of American and Chinese intelligence officers in Chungking.[6] The American representative on SACO was Navy Captain Milton Miles,[7] while the Chinese representative was General Tai Li, who was Generalissimo Chiang Kai-Shek's chief of intelligence. General Tai Li wielded immense power in all aspects of Chinese government and politics. When Nicol Smith arrived in Chungking, Captain Miles offered him some advice: "To get anything done in China you have to work with Tai Li . . . Otherwise he can and will delay you in a thousand ways . . . . For numerous reasons the General has a natural suspicion of any clandestine work carried on by a foreign country.[8]

JCS Directive 245 provided that SACO, which was directed by General Tai Li, had to approve all clandestine operations from China into Thailand. Tai Li therefore held absolute control of operations directed into Thailand and also over the dissemination of much of the intelligence collected on Southeast Asia. Chinese obstructionist tactics often handicapped OSS operations into Thailand and Indochina. No real progress was possible until the OSS intelligence base was moved from China (in 1944) and out of SACO's control.[9]

China was not the only "ally" to cause problems in the conduct of intelligence operations into Thailand. Conflict between the United States and England had been mounting since the decision was made to support the Thai operation. The conflict had its roots in the difference of opinion at the highest levels of government as to whether Thailand should be treated as an occupied ally (the American view) or as an enemy (the British view). The anti-colonial position of the United States also entered into this difference in policies. The War Department viewed the situation with alarm: "By the summer of 1943 OSS-British relations were so bad that [OSS operations] were in danger of being eliminated."[10]

The OSS and the SOE were both engaged in a spirited competition to develop a Thai intelligence network. The competition precluded real cooperation until the last year of the war. At that time it became apparent that the two intelligence organizations would gain from joint planning and operations. This atmosphere of Allied "cooperation" made it difficult for their intelligence agencies to coordinate activities that might have helped speed attempts to achieve communications with the resistance leadership inside Thailand.

THAI AGENTS GAIN SPONSORSHIP AND MOVE FROM ENGLAND TO INDIA

The desire of the Thai students in England to serve in the war effort was in consonance with requirements levied on British intelligence agencies. England, unlike the United States, had to determine whether to return its Thai residents to Bangkok or to allow them to remain in England. At first the Thais were denied permission to join the British armed forces. However the government did allow them to join the Pioneer Corps, formed of residents of Axis countries living in England.[11] The Thais disliked intensely the menial labor chores they were given in the Pioneer Corps and abhorred the stigma attached to their enforced status as enemy aliens.

Finally, at the urging of SOE, beginning in August 1942 Thai citizens were permitted to volunteer for service in the British army. They had to meet regular military physical standards, which resulted in the elimination of many volunteers. Eventually thirty-seven Thais were accepted for service in a special unit that was then "loaned" to SOE for training and operations.

After six months of intelligence training the group, under the Thai command of Major Arun, reached India in January 1943 (a roster of the unit is given in the appendices). After arrival in India fourteen of the men were assigned to other duties. The remaining twenty-three operated under the control of SOE, which operated in Asia under the code name Force 136.

Force 136 conducted operations into Malaya and the Netherlands East Indies from Ceylon, while operations into Burma, Indochina, and Thailand were directed from Calcutta. The Thai agents were placed under the control of the Siam Country Section, commanded by Major A. C. (Peter) Pointon.[12] The Thai group nicknamed themselves "White Elephants" (Chang Phuak), an appellation each member cherished throughout the war.[13] Force 136 established as its top priority the determination by its agents whether a Thai resistance organization had been formed in Thailand and, if so, its size, status, and disposition toward the Allies.[14]

Force 136 established the White Elephants as its primary intelligence collection and infiltration element targeted at Thailand. Sir Andrew Gilchrist has described British intelligence operations with the group in his 1970 book *Bangkok: Top Secret*, cited frequently herein.

Another collection unit was formed in case the Thai population and its underground leadership were hostile to the British. The second element was composed of Chinese of Thai descent recruited primarily in southern China. In keeping with the British intelligence system of coding their agent teams with the names of colors, the Chinese agents became "Reds" and "Blues" to match the Seri Thai "Whites." Little has been published in English concerning the activities of the Chinese teams. Ten Reds were trained in India for use on Thai operations, while a second group (the Blues) were under training when the war ended.[15]

By the summer of 1943 the United States was actively planning to infiltrate Thailand with Thai agents overland from southern China, while the British planned to send their agents to Thailand by air or sea. All of those plans were made without firm knowledge that an underground existed inside Thailand. In August 1943, however, came the welcome news that a resistance movement was operating in Thailand. The underground succeeded in sending three senior members from Bangkok to Chungking with this information. Details of this successful operation are discussed later in this chapter.

EXPANSION OF THE SERI THAI MOVEMENT IN THAILAND

Pridi Banomyong's small group of resistance leaders worked under unusual conditions. While they were not constantly harassed by the Phibun government, it was advisable to keep their activities secret from both the Japanese and the Thais outside their circle. The X.O. Group grew slowly and its influence expanded. Membership varied but in actual numbers the group remained small, apparently under ten. Discrepancies in membership listings probably are due to security precautions. Various members of the top leadership echelon were uncertain as to the exact status of other members. Many members in the second level of leadership did not know, until almost the end of the war, that Pridi was the leader of the combined resistance movement.

One of the most reliable accounts of early membership in the X.O. Group was provided by Chamkat Phalangkun. His roster included the following men and their positions in late 1942: Pridi Banomyong, member of the Council of Regents; Phraongchao Athitthaya Thip-apha, president of the Council of Regents (his presence is disputed by others); Khuang Aphaiwong, minister of commerce; Thawi Bunyaket, secretary to the Cabinet; Navy Captain Luang Suphachalasai, vice minister of communications; Duean Bunnak, vice minister of education; Rear Admiral Luang Sangwon Yuthakit, vice commander of the navy; Louis Banomyong, Pridi's brother, treasurer of the X.O. Group; and Chamkat Phalangkun, secretary of the X.O. Group.[16] An additional number of persons apparently were close to this inner circle of leadership, although probably not members of the X.O. Group. They included several senior civil servants and about ten members of the National Assembly.

Significantly, at this early stage of organization, there were no army or police officials in high leadership positions in the X.O. Group. Pridi continued to rely on close friends and acquaintances who had long been associated with him and whose loyalty was unquestioned. There was no attempt actively to recruit underground leaders whose political reliability and friendship were questionable and of short association with Pridi. This reliance on friendship and the strength of the Royal Thai Navy continued as a trait of Pridi's leadership in the postwar period and culminated in his navy-supported final attempt to regain power that resulted in failure and his exile.

Membership of the X.O. Group varied with the times; as new men gained access to the highest levels of underground leadership others were shifted to make room for them. Malai's list of early members of the X.O. Group, for example, included those given by Chamkat with the addition of Major General M.L. Kri Dechati-wong.[17] This was the first mention of an army officer in the X.O. Group. The exigencies of resistance activity and revised shifts of power in the last two years of the war also brought about changes at the top level of leadership. By the end of the war Pridi had reorga-nized his high command several times. In a speech to the Seri Thai after the end of the war he specifically thanked by name and position these men in the X.O. Group: Thawi Bunyaket; Admiral Sangwon Yuthakit; Captain Luang Suphachalasai; General Chit Mansin Sinatyotharak; Direk Chaiyanam; and Police General Adun Adundecharat.[18]

Whatever the exact membership, the X.O. Group directed a constantly growing underground that expanded through natural inclinations as well as direct recruitment. As reported later in the war, the growth of the underground came about because:

After the Japanese invasion, Thai resentment found expression in the spontaneous formation of small groups of non-collaborationists

. . . . these groups gradually made contact with each other, merged, and set up an underground organization with a central executive committee . . . Supporting this committee are lesser officials and non-officials who can carry out the orders of the executive committee and can oppose the Japanese and the Phibul regime more actively because their positions are less prominent and their movements less under surveillance.[19]

Originally Pridi called the underground the "Movement for Siamese Liberation."[20] Betrayal of early plans for the establishment of a free government in northern Thailand was only the first lesson in security the underground learned. The members practiced strict security and compartmentation (separation of elements within the movement to lessen the amount of information a man could divulge if captured). Malai recorded that "all agreed that it was better for one to die than for the group to perish."[21]

The morale of the Thai resistance movement increased significantly when broadcasts from KGIA in San Francisco reported that Thais abroad had started resistance activities. While the broadcasts could be received in Thailand only on short-wave radios, the information had special meaning to the X.O. Group. News that M.R. Seni had repudiated the declaration of war and had started a firm anti-Japanese resistance movement was of incalculable importance. One of Pridi's first priorities was to make contact with the Thai resistance groups sponsored by the Allies.

The resistance movement in Thailand faced a massive job of organization. In addition to the primary need to establish contact with the Allies, Pridi saw his objectives as four-fold. First, to recruit members in all areas of Thailand to expand the organization's effectiveness. Second, to obtain food, arms, and equipment from all available sources. Third, to replace government figures with men sympathetic to the resistance movement, particularly in the provinces where the resistance would need to expand. Fourth, to win over the loyalties of the National Police and the army which at the time were firmly behind Phibun.[22] The main thrust of the Seri Thai was to organize itself into an effective agency for active resistance and to prepare to wage guerrilla war against the Japanese.

As Pridi moved forward with organizational efforts, encouraged by news of the formation of resistance movements abroad, he was acutely aware of two essential requirements that only the Allies could provide. He required military equipment, arms, and training for his forces. But more important, he needed recognition by the Allies that Thailand had not supported the Phibun government's declaration of war. The resistance leadership was united in their view that an active resistance movement would be the most effective way to demonstrate loyalty to the Allies and a commitment to democracy.

Without arms, equipment, and training, the resistance could not conduct guerrilla operations against the Japanese. In 1942 and 1943 the resistance movement in Thailand was still a small elite cadre united in its political views and opposition to the Japanese, but with no operational capability to actively oppose the occupying Japanese forces. It was vital that the members expand their numbers, gain a minimal organizational cohesion, and acquire the military power to combat the Japanese. The group devoted its efforts to expand the network of cadres and the underground outside Bangkok, and to organize an intelligence network. Pridi correctly assumed that contact with the Allies would result in a need for intelligence on Japanese forces in Thailand as well as those moving into Burma and Malaya.

Since Thailand was officially allied with Japan, military and political leaders of the two countries held frequent discussions on policy and plans. Thai officials obtained valuable information about Japanese war plans and strategy that was later sent to the Allies.[23] Furthermore, as travel and trade increased between Thailand and Japan, Thai officials obtained information on potential bombing targets in Japan, internal political developments, and the opinions of Japanese officials and citizens.[24] This information on Japan was to become important when communications were finally established with the Allies. The resistance also gathered considerable information on Japanese military activity in Thailand by watching daily events and listening to public announcements.

A second way the Thai underground assisted the Allied war effort began prior to the establishment of communications. This concerned the issue of how to handle and interrogate Allied prisoners of war (POW). An agreement between Japan and Thailand, reached shortly after the Thai declaration of war, provided that the forces of each country maintained physical control of POW and others apprehended by their forces.[25] This provided two channels for handling Allied personnel. Civilians were interned in Thai facilities that were adequate if spartan. As Allied airmen and Thai agents fell into the hands of the Thai police and military forces, they too were controlled by the Thai constabulary. On the other hand, Allied forces captured in the conquest of Malaya and Singapore, and later moved to Thailand as laborers to construct the notorious "death railroad" to Burma, remained under Japanese control.

As the war progressed the Thais made every effort to keep captured Allied personnel out of Japanese hands. They initiated a clandestine policy by which Allied pilots and Thai agents were given all possible assistance and whisked to safety without the knowledge of the Japanese.[26] The agreement allowed Japanese to interrogate POW controlled by Thai agencies, but only in the presence of a Thai official and never with the use of torture. This policy had particular significance for the infiltration of Thai agents.

A third series of activities by the underground was to be of particular benefit to Allied infiltration efforts. A concentrated effort to locate and record for future use possible routes of infiltration for Allied agents and military forces produced valuable data for intelligence operations. The Seri Thai planned drop zones where men and equipment could be parachuted safely and in secrecy. They also charted routes for overland movements and located sites along the coasts of the Gulf of Thailand and the Andaman Sea where seaplanes could land or submarines surface free from Japanese detection. These activities, well underway by February 1943, were concentrated in southern Thailand between Hua Hin, Bang Phapan, and Huai Sak. To assist in supporting future air, sea, and land infiltration, the early resistance cadre recruited a number of supporters among the local population and civil service. These support agents received superficial training on how to bury parachutes and what to do when "mysterious strangers" appeared in their isolated villages.[27]

There does not appear at first to have been a planned program for sabotage of Japanese facilities or assassination of their personnel. Later in the war such activities were more controlled. However, throughout the war individuals and small groups of Thai acting on their own conducted small-scale acts of harassment. Lone Japanese soldiers frequently were beaten or killed, gasoline and food supplies contaminated or stolen. The Thai people conducted these and other similar actions to demonstrate in a concrete manner their opposition to the Japanese occupation.

These small acts of harassment were generally carried out spontaneously when the opportunity arose—usually in response to a lack of vigilance on the part of Japanese guards or carelessness by Japanese soldiers.

When larger opportunities appeared, officials took advantage of them. For example, a stationmaster in Bangkok drove a train engine and four cars loaded with ammunition into the Chao Phraya River. Japanese response was swift and harsh: the stationmaster was executed.[28] Yet these minor acts of harassment buoyed Thai spirits and increased the cost to the Japanese of occupying Thailand.

THAI EFFORTS TO COMMUNICATE WITH THE ALLIES

Efforts to contact the Allies began early in the war. The Thais lacked both the powerful communications system needed to broadcast information to China or India and access to the international mails. Therefore the resistance leadership in Bangkok decided that the only effective way to contact the Allies was to send a high-ranking member from their leadership level on an overland journey to China.

Their first attempt to send a man out of Thailand was made in late 1942. Chaowong Saensiriphan, national assemblyman from Phrae province and one of Pridi's closest personal friends, sent a seven-man party into Laos in an attempt to reach southern China. The men disappeared without a trace, as did four more men sent three months later.[29] It is unknown whether they were captured and executed by Japanese forces, tribesmen, or Chinese agents, or died from hardships encountered in their travels.

Early in 1943 the underground made a second major attempt to exfiltrate Chamkat Phalangkun to China. Chamkat, a powerful member of the National Assembly as well as a member of the X.O. Group, had the stature Pridi felt was needed to persuade the Allies to aid the Thai resistance effort with arms and material and to give it political support. Chamkat was to leave Thailand, ostensibly on a trip to Japan, and then travel overland through Indochina to Chungking.[30] Malai Chupanit's book *X.O. Group* covers this journey by Chamkat in great detail and includes valuable information on the political travails he faced on arrival in China.

Chamkat was to present the following points for the Allies' consideration. First, the Thais wanted to annul the declaration of war because it was promulgated contrary to the Thai constitution and against the will of the people. Second, a spirit of friendship and non-aggression between Thailand and the Allies should continue. Chamkat was to emphasize that Thai troops had not fired on Allied forces. Third, England was requested to reconsider its harsh political stance toward Thailand. The United States and England were requested to fund and support the Thai resistance movement so it could conduct guerrilla warfare against Japanese forces in Thailand. Finally, in the event the proposals were accepted, Pridi wanted to be evacuated by seaplane so he could establish a Thai government-in-exile. Acceptance of the proposals should be broadcast over Radio Chungking, Radio Delhi, or by the British Broadcasting Corporation.

Chamkat received a visa through the assistance of the French embassy in Bangkok to travel through Indochina to Japan for "training." He left Bangkok on 28 February 1943 on a journey that required two months for him to reach Chungking (via Laos, Hanoi, and Lieuchow). Immediately upon his arrival in China, Tai Li's group placed Chamkat in "protective custody" (a euphemism for house arrest) and closely monitored his activities.

Chamkat wrote numerous letters and sent many telegrams to M.R. Seni, the U.S. State Department, and the British Foreign Office. Available information indicates that the Chinese closely controlled his communications and apparently deliberately failed to deliver important messages between Chamkat and other resistance leaders in the West. Chamkat spent over three months in Chungking trying to meet representatives of British or American intelligence agencies before Tai Li admitted to Captain Miles that a senior Thai resistance officer was in China. Nicol Smith, Colonel Khap, and the Thai agents trying to infiltrate Thailand did not know Chamkat had arrived safely in China until midsummer 1943. M.R. Seni first learned of Chamkat's arrival in China on 3 April 1943. Unfortunately he did not know Chamkat personally, or whom he represented. Attempts at detailed communications between the two men were stymied by the Chinese and by errors in judgment in Washington, D.C. Apparently the zealous concern for security slowed recognition of a genuine representative of the Thai resistance. Several messages between Seni and Chamkat, especially one that should have established Chamkat's bona fides beyond doubt, were never delivered. Only after many weeks had passed was Chamkat finally able to convince M.R. Seni that he did represent the resistance organization in Thailand. By then both OSS and Seni had determined that Chamkat should immediately come to Washington for a thorough debriefing. That request was stalled by Chinese intelligence and it was not until August 1943 that Tai Li agreed to permit Chamkat to leave China.

During the frustrating exchange of communications the Chinese gradually relaxed some of the stringent security around Chamkat. When his importance was realized, both American and British intelligence representatives in China attempted to arrange meetings with him. Accounts of this period are jumbled and it is difficult to determine when such meetings finally took place. Captain Miles apparently was the first outsider to meet Chamkat. The first Seri Thai man to contact Chamkat was Major Arun, who had been sent by Force 136 after they received word that an exfiltrator was in China.

By that time both the British and American governments had received and reacted to the information and requests Chamkat had sent to the West. Thus Major Arun was able to inform Chamkat that communications had been established and that most of the Seri Thai requests had been favorably received. However England summarily disapproved the request for a government-in-exile.

Major Arun was bitter at the cavalier treatment Chamkat had received at the hands of the Chinese. He was able to arrange meetings between Chamkat and other Western intelligence officers. While the meetings had been long delayed, they were valuable. Chamkat provided Major Arun with details on Pridi's organization in Thailand and Major Arun passed on details for British plans to infiltrate Thailand. Through Major Arun the British furnished Chamkat with a system for clandestine communications with Pridi. It was a microdot message affixed to an old Thai 100-baht banknote, and contained details of Force 136 plans to spirit members of the X.O. Group out of Thailand for consultations. Force 136 hoped that Chamkat had sufficient connections to get the message overland to Pridi along his route of travel to China. Force 136 sent the communication without any information on Chamkat's situation and made the effort on a gamble it might succeed. Apparently the message was never delivered to Pridi. British forces kept the pick-up rendezvous mentioned in the microdot but there was no response from the Thai.

Major Arun apparently kept Captain Miles and Colonel Khap informed of the details of his conversations with Chamkat. Information reached the United States on the gist of their discussions. But the Chinese constantly frustrated Colonel Khap's attempts to see Chamkat in person. Captain Miles also was unable to arrange a meeting between the two Thai resistance figures. Malai laid the blame for the deplorable state of affairs on confusion and wartime security, and described with understatement what must have been an extremely frustrating situation: ". . . strict regulations and roles . . . were so secure that it was impossible [for Chamkat] to meet with M.L. Khap until they were certain over who was who in Chungking, and at that time almost nobody knew who was who."[31]

In the midst of this confused situation came news that two more Thai representatives had arrived in Chungking. The Chinese quickly isolated them, just as they had Chamkat. They were not permitted to meet Chamkat or other Allied intelligence officers. It was some time before Tai Li permitted Allied representatives to see the newcomers. Chamkat, by then ill and completely frustrated, wrote a long report on the Thai resistance that he delivered with a poignant cover letter pleading for assistance to Thailand. The lengthy report detailed the opposition to the Phibun government's wartime policies, outlined the formation and organization of the X.O. Group and underground, and reported on their activities. The letter and report reached OSS headquarters in Washington intact and served as the first accurate information delivered to the U.S. about the resistance movement inside Thailand.

Soon afterwards Chamkat died, allegedly of stomach cancer. He had been frustrated in his attempts to reach the West to link the Thai resistance with the Allies. Although he did not know it, his reports, cables, and letters were the first accounts of the Thai resistance movement to reach the Allies. His estimate that the internal resistance movement had the support of most of the people and a preponderance of the military and civilian police forces was extremely important to American political leaders. His revelation that Pridi Banomyong, the royal regent, was the leader of the resistance movement galvanized the overseas Seri Thai as well as their Allied sponsors. They all realized that if such a high-ranking Thai official could direct the underground without detection, the movement had great potential and deserved support.

So although Chamkat died before personally seeing his mission to fruition, he nevertheless succeeded in convincing the Allies of the viability of the Thai resistance effort. This new attitude of the Allies led to the provision of the arms, equipment, and training necessary for ultimate success. Malai called Chamkat "The Knight of the Round Table of the Seri Thai."[32] After the war, when others could come forward, many Thai and Allied leaders eulogized Chamkat's contributions to the Thai resistance movement.

A major question is: why was this first attempt by Thai resistance leaders to contact the Allies so poorly handled by the Allies? Four valuable months were wasted in establishing a link between Thailand and the Allies because of duplicity and lack of cooperation. The wasted time meant loss of valuable intelligence on Japanese activities and handicapped effective intelligence operations. Much of the blame for this state of affairs falls on the shoulders of the Chinese intelligence chief, General Tai Li. Apparently he deliberately failed to forward Chamkat's letters in a timely and complete manner. This action can be attributed to a perception of different national interests or to an attempt to increase his personal power. It certainly prevented valuable information from reaching the Allies. More delay occurred because M.R. Seni was slow to recognize Chamkat's importance. The extent to which Seni was appraised of Chamkat's value and knowledge is open to question. It is possible that American diplomatic or intelligence officials did not give M.R. Seni all available details. The diary that Seni kept during his stay in Washington is replete with references to Chamkat and his own efforts to contact Chamkat. It appears that once the Allies became convinced of Chamkat's importance, every effort was made to bring him to the United States. By then it was too late, however, and Chamkat's untimely death prevented the Allies from obtaining valuable insights into the situation inside Thailand. The entire episode was instrumental in the decision to move OSS operations out of southern China and out of Tai Li's control.

ALLIED-THAI MEETINGS IN CHUNGKING

Pridi assumed that Chamkat had failed to reach China after months passed without word from him. For security reasons the Allies did not broadcast word of Chamkat's arrival in Chungking. In the absence of news Pridi sent yet another team of government officials, the fourth, to China. The two men of this team were Sa-nguan Tularak, a member of the National Assembly and chief of the Bureau of Tobacco Monopoly, Ministry of Finance, and Daeng Khunadilok (also referred to as Daeng Tilaka), chief of the Press Bureau, Ministry of Foreign Affairs. Both individuals were long-time Pridi associates. They left Bangkok in July 1943 for Chungking and followed a route similar to that taken by Chamkat.[33]

The arrival in Chungking of two more representatives from Thailand was a fortuitous event in light of the disappointments of the Chamkat experience. After some difficulty and frustration, Allied intelligence personnel were able to meet with the men. As a result they made the basic decisions to support fully the Thai resistance movement.

After the Chamkat fiasco General Tai Li was more generous in allowing Allied representatives to talk with this Thai delegation. Captain Miles, Colonel Khap, and Major Arun were all able to meet with the two men. M.L. Khap was particularly anxious to see them because he had been denied the chance to meet Chamkat. He was desperate for information needed to plan the overland infiltration of the Thai agents under his command.[34]

These Chungking meetings were crucial to the success of the Thai resistance movement. Sa-nguan and Daeng emphasized that the resistance movement had the support of the people and most of the members of the National Assembly. They reported that the resistance also had military support and potential for guerrilla operations if supplied with additional arms and equipment. Finally, the two men reported that the resistance had a viable intelligence-gathering and psychological warfare capability.[35]

All parties to the talks agreed on several points that were to form the basis for resistance operations into Thailand. First, the Allies would "consider" Pridi's request for evacuation to establish a government-in-exile. England was adamantly opposed to this step and it never received further consideration. The Allies agreed to support the resistance movement with weapons, equipment, and delivery aircraft. China would provide facilities from which OSS could launch operations into Thailand and Indochina, a commitment which was freely ignored by the Chinese when it suited their purposes.[36]

The Thai and OSS considered it critical that Sa-nguan and Daeng go to the United States for more detailed debriefings and to meet with resistance leaders. Their travel from Chungking would also remove them from Chinese control. OSS provided the funds to finance their trip to Washington. From there the two men flew to England to brief local Seri Thai members. Eventually Sa-nguan went to Ceylon where he supported American intelligence operations until the end of the war.[37]

Events of the summer of 1943 stimulated the Thai resistance effort and were immensely valuable to later operations in Thailand. The efforts of Chamkat, Sa-nguan, and Daeng brought the first knowledge that a potentially powerful resistance movement existed in Thailand. Furthermore, their overland journeys showed that infiltration into Thailand was possible. Most importantly, the Allies finalized plans to support the Thai resistance movement with arms and equipment, a step essential for effective guerrilla operations.

FIELD MARSHAL PHIBUN'S INITIATIVES WITH THE ALLIES

Most historical accounts of World War II place Marshal Phibun in the villain's role because of his cooperation and subsequent alliance with the Japanese. Phibun governed as a dictator and was unpopular because of his regimented and at times repressive policies. But in fairness to Phibun, his relationship with the Japanese was in Thailand's best interests. His reasons for joining Thailand's interests with those of Japan have been described. At the start of the war it appeared that Japan would win, and Phibun felt it essential for Thailand to be on the victor's side.

As the war years brought increasing setbacks to Japan, especially starting in 1943, Phibun took steps to insure that Thailand would land "on its feet" no matter who won the war. As early as 1942, when discussing war plans with Colonel Net Khemayothin, then plans officer for the Thai Army Field Forces, Phibun stated with pragmatism, "Khun Net, which side do you think will lose this war? That side is our enemy."[38]

Anti-Japanese elements within the Royal Thai Army began attempts to contact the Allies in early 1942. The Northwest Army (Kong Thap Phayap), formed shortly after the alliance with Japan, acted as the focus for such efforts. The Northwest Army, whose mission was to protect the Japanese northern flank, was stationed in northern Thailand and the annexed area of Burma. The army, particularly elements of its Third Division, clashed sporadically with the Chinese Ninety-third Division along the ill-defined border between Yunnan and Chiang Tung (the Thai name for Burma's Keng Tung province). Several officers, seeing an opportunity to establish friendly contacts with the Chinese, approached Phibun with their idea. Phibun directed that a plan be carried out to do so, beginning what Net described as one of the most secret operations of the Thai war effort.[39]

At the start of the war Phibun enjoyed the complete loyalty of the Royal Thai Army. It formed the basis for his personal and political power and its membership benefited from their loyalty. The army's loyalty was personal—it supported Phibun but not necessarily the onerous Japanese occupation of Thailand. When called on, the army augmented Japanese military plans but seldom did Thai military units engage Allied forces in battle. The sporadic clashes along the China-Burma border were as much a conflict between hereditary enemies as support of Japanese interests.

The Thai army was not strong enough to fight the massive Japanese military power in Thailand without outside assistance. In the early years they were not able to offer more than token spirited opposition to the Japanese. The army's leadership was primarily concerned with avoiding the catastrophe of disarmament by the Japanese, and therefore carried out those policies necessary to comply with Japanese orders.

The bulk of the Thai army's military power was shifted north, away from Bangkok, after Japan moved its own military forces into the country. Through years of introspective leadership and indoctrination the army had developed a sense of cohesion and strength. Although factions had developed, the overall strength of the army lay in its ability to respond to leadership with alacrity and loyal obedience. The members of the chain of command, particularly in the senior ranks, were loyal to Phibun. He in turn installed his most trusted associates in influential command positions, who then in turn developed a chain of loyal subordinates. When the chain of command broke (as happened when Phibun lost the Prime Minister's Office), the chain of loyalty within the army merely flowed to the next lower commander. It was a system that fostered cohesiveness and response that was to serve the country well. The deputy commander in chief, General Chit Mansin Sinatyotharak, became a powerful and trusted member of Pridi's X.O. Group.

Phibun transferred several officers to new assignments to facilitate his plan to achieve contact with the Chinese. Lieutenant General (LTG) Chira Wichitsongkhram became commander of the

Northwest Army. Chira, who had exerted enormous influence in his prior position as chief of staff of the army Field Forces, in turn assigned Major General (MG) Luang Han Songkhram as commander of the Third Division in Keng Tung. Another close associate, Net Khemayothin, was entrusted with the delicate tasks of planning and conducting the secret talks.

General Han attempted the first contact with the Chinese in January 1944, when he sent a three-man party to the border area with a letter for the Ninety-third Division commander. The Thai party delivered the message to the Chinese under a white truce flag in the middle of the Lam River that forms the borders of Burma and China. The Thai party, consisting of Lieutenant Colonel (LTC) Sawaeng Thapphasut, LTC At Na Bangchang, and Captain Saman Wirawaithaya, met with a Chinese delegation on 5 January 1944. Brigadier General (BG) Lu Wi Eng, commander of the Ninety-third Division, headed the Chinese team.

Since neither side had the authority to speak at the policy level for their respective governments, the discussions were general and exploratory.[40] The Thai requested that their efforts be made known to British and American representatives in Chungking. The meeting was friendly, and both sides made tentative plans for future meetings at which the delegations would have greater authority to negotiate matters of common interest. LTG Chira personally briefed Phibun on the meeting when the group returned to Bangkok.

The Chinese informed other Allies of the contact on the Lam River, including Nicol Smith and Colonel Khap. M.L. Khap immediately wrote a discreet letter to LTC Sawaeng, who once had been his student. He requested information from Sawaeng about anti-Japanese activity in Thailand, but did not mention the presence in China of the OSS-trained Thai agents. The letter was delivered to front-line Thai positions, which passed it in turn to Sawaeng, MG Han, LTG Chira, and to Marshal Phibun. Phibun, who had assigned M.L. Khap to the Thai Legation in the United States, learned of his protege's presence in China and must have concluded that some type of anti-Japanese activity sponsored by Americans was underway. Colonel Khap did not outline the details of his mission to China, but Phibun must have understood the significance of the letter. It was the first communication from the Allies to Thailand's official government. Phibun and the military men by whom the letter was passed kept it a secret.

The Chinese also delivered a request for a future meeting to expand on the initiatives established at the first meeting on the Lam River. Phibun, personally delivering M.L. Khap's letter to General Chira, told him to arrange another meeting and to select his delegates. General Chira chose Colonel Net to lead the Thai delegation. Though Net was not the senior member of the delegation in terms of military rank, he was specifically designated by Phibun as his authorized spokesman. Other members were MG Han, LTC Krachang Phonphoem, LTC Sawaeng, and Captain Sawan.

The delegation left for the meeting site on the Lam River in late March 1944 and the conference was held 2 April. Net carried both a letter of authorization from Phibun and the prime minister's personal gift to General Lu, a beautifully engraved hunting rifle. Police Lieutenant Thani Sathonkit, a Chinese linguist and skilled intelligence officer, joined the meeting at the last minute. Thani was the personal representative of Police General Adun. His presence provides firm evidence that Phibun and Adun were both aware of the significance of the meeting. However, there is no evidence that would connect Adun's knowledge of the meeting plans with Pridi's resistance movement.

General Lu again headed the second Chinese delegation. Significantly, there were no representatives of the American or Thai groups in China. Although M.L. Khap knew that another meeting was to be held, and had prepared the letter that led to the meeting, the Chinese did not inform either him or Nicol Smith about it. General Lu told the surprised Thai delegation, who had expected M.L. Khap, that he had planned to come but had been called back at the last minute to Chungking on urgent business.[41] Smith and Khap were anguished and frustrated at this Chinese duplicity. It was another example of Chinese obstructionism, officially described after the war in this way: "All American activity in China suffered from the soporific atmosphere pervading Chungking officialdom. Personal self-interest and corruption, as well as the partisan rather than national policy . . . negated any efficient conduct of active warfare against Japan."[42]

The April meeting between the Thais and Chinese was more important than the first one. The two delegations agreed on various important issues: 1) Thailand wanted the United States, England, and the Seri Thai informed of the Thai delegation's participation; 2) The Chinese and Thais agreed to establish mutual communications; 3) Both sides agreed to cease border crossing operations and incidents involving military forces; 4) The Thais asked that Allied bombers attack only Japanese military targets in their raids against Thailand; and 5) Thailand was told for the first time that the Allies were formulating a major plan for land and sea operations against the Japanese forces in Thailand and Malaya. The Allied command promised to keep the Thais informed and to tell them when the plan would be implemented.[43] The last item was the most important issue, and one of great significance to the Thai delegation. They asserted that their forces would join the Allies in any anti-Japanese operations in Thailand.

Colonel Net and LTG Chira briefed Phibun on the results of the second meeting with the Chinese. Among the items requiring final approval by Phibun was a Chinese request to send political and military representatives to meet with Chiang Kai-Shek in Chungking. This was to be the third in the series of meetings between the two countries. Phibun selected Police General Adun as chief of the delegation, and also Colonel Prayun Phamonmontri, MG Han Songkhram, and Colonel Net.[44] Colonel Prayun is described as one of the most ardent pro-Japanese officers in the Thai army. He was to act as Phibun's political affairs representative.

The two meetings on the China-Burma border, and plans for a third meeting in Chungking, reflect directly the political environment of the period and Marshal Phibun's role in anti-Japanese activity. Thai sources report that Phibun was involved in or directly knowledgeable of contacts with the Allies as early as 1942. He was intimately involved in directing such activities by 1944. During these years he was outwardly posturing as the pro-Japanese puppet prime minister. Phibun's concern for the welfare of his country has been cited as the primary reason he claims to have allied Thailand with Japan.

Phibun spent most of the war years in an extremely delicate balancing act. He overtly espoused the Japanese cause and covertly directed contacts with the Allies. He engaged in anti-Japanese activity at the same time that his liberal opponents were sending representatives to China. By 1944 Phibun was fully aware that the Allies were actively planning for military operations into Thailand. He had committed himself and his nation's armed forces to participation in such anti-Japanese operations. Furthermore, Phibun realized from M.L. Khap's letter to Sawaeng that some Allied resistance activity was forming in southern China.

There is no available documentation that indicates that either the United States or England was aware of Phibun's participation in the program of meetings between China and the Thai Northwest Army. Nicol Smith and M.L. Khap knew about the Thai army's participation. But they may not have been aware that Phibun had directed the Thai efforts to that end. A plausible case can be made for the conjecture that Phibun's role in the Thai-Chinese meetings was known at least to the Chinese (from Phibun's gift of the rifle to General Lu, if for no other reason). Whether that information was passed to the Americans in Chungking is a matter of speculation.

Phibun, in addition to having extensive knowledge about anti-Japanese plans and activities, had an active observer inside the domestic resistance movement, Police General Adun Adundecharat. He was a man with great power in the Phibun government and a close personal and political ally of the prime minister. General Adun was, in many ways, the most interesting figure in the resistance movement. Phibun appointed General Adun as his chief of intelligence. Phibun's wife has told of her husband's role in directing General Adun's anti-Japanese activities.[45] Thanphuying La-iat Phibunsongkhram claimed that Adun reported almost daily to Phibun during the war.

As will be shown in future chapters, Adun was intimately and significantly involved in supporting the infiltration of Thai agents into the country. He also provided security for Thai and Allied intelligence operations throughout Thailand. Although Adun did not enter Pridi's formal leadership circle until 1944, he rose rapidly to become Pridi's deputy in charge of the entire resistance movement. Thanpuying La-iat has stated that Adun provided Phibun with detailed reports on the activities of the Thai agents who later arrived inside Thailand.[46] Phibun was aware of most of the innermost details of Pridi's resistance movement. He knew of the policies and activities of the movement, the identities of most of the resistance leaders, and of the presence of Allied agents in Bangkok. Despite the personal rivalry between Phibun and Pridi, and the national political implications of this competition, Phibun did not try to neutralize members of the Thai resistance leadership. He had imprisoned several political opponents, but he did not take advantage of the information obtained from General Adun to eliminate his foremost political rivals.

This information places Phibun's activities and policies during the war in a new perspective. Phibun led the Japanese to believe, through his public pronouncements and actions, that he was their ally. At the same time he was furthering the interests of Thailand and giving support to Allied plans to engage in open combat against the Japanese. Thanphuying La-iat justifiably asserts that Phibun's behind-the-scenes support of resistance activities constitutes indisputable evidence that Phibun's government had no intention whatever of aligning itself with Japan militarily or politically.[47]

While Phibun was not a member of Pridi's resistance movement, he contributed to its successes. Phibun's decision not to betray the resistance movement to the Japanese saved the resistance movement and the lives of its members. Although Phibun was later arrested and tried by the postwar Pridi government as a war criminal, Pridi did not press this issue. Phibun was acquitted of all charges against him. If Pridi was unaware of Phibun's covert knowledge and support of resistance activity during the war, he knew of his role after the war. General Adun, who could have kept Pridi informed of Phibun's knowledge if he had so chosen, kept secret Phibun's extensive information on the resistance movement.

At the same time Phibun was arranging for the meetings with the Chinese, he ordered Colonel Net to prepare plans to use Phetchabun province as a last stronghold against the Japanese after the Allied attack was launched into Thailand. He believed that Thai participation in such an offensive would force Japan to remove the Thai government and to disarm the Thai armed forces. Phibun began plans for an alternate command post for himself as well as for a civilian capital that could serve as a sanctuary for key members of the government. The Thai Army Field Forces headquarters in Phetchabun was charged with carrying out the plan to move the capital from Bangkok.[48]

The plan to move the capital to Phetchabun was based on reasonable strategic grounds, but only if one had the knowledge Phibun possessed of the real probability of war between Thailand and Japan. It is unknown whether or not these strategic considerations were shared with resistance leaders. Most likely, the majority of the civilian government and resistance membership knew only that Phibun proposed to move, at great cost, the Thai capital from the comforts of Bangkok to a remote and malaria-ridden valley.

Pridi and his followers used Phibun's plan as an excuse to seize power from him. Pridi rallied his supporters in the National Assembly and defeated the legislation that would provide for moving the capital to the north. Phibun resigned as prime minister, and later as commander in chief of the armed forces. His defeat resulted in abandonment of the plan to send a delegation to meet with Chiang Kai-Shek.

The events that led to Phibun's resignation were primarily political; the issue of the resistance was of secondary importance. Many of Phibun's closest associates later took major positions in the resistance movement, most notably Police General Adun and Army Deputy Commander General Chit Mansin Sinatyotharak.

Net viewed Phibun in a sympathetic light. A strong supporter of Phibun, but even more a supporter of Thai sovereignty, Net transferred his loyalty to Pridi. He was not aware until later of Pridi's influence and leadership in the resistance movement. Of Phibun, Net later said:

> As far as Marshal Phibunsongkhram was concerned . . . he had to strive to live with Japan, which had invaded the country, in order to

be able to preserve the freedom of the Thai people. At the same time he had to attempt to preserve the strength of the Thai armed forces and prevent the Japanese forces from disarming the Thai military.[49]

Nuechterlein observed, "in fairness to Pibun [sic] it should be stated that he was no . . . friend of the Japanese during the war years."[50]

CONCLUSION

The period 1942 to 1944 was both productive and frustrating for all elements of the Thai resistance movement. There were major advances in organization among all sections of the Seri Thai. The most important factor in the Allies' determination to support the resistance was information about Pridi's movement that had finally reached them. At the same time the handicap of inadequate communications became obvious. The Allies were tantalized with the potential for intelligence waiting inside Thailand but were not yet able to exploit the presence of Pridi's resistance movement. Pridi knew that the Allies probably were waiting to communicate with Thailand but could not gain information about his attempts to send representatives to China.

By early 1944 a number of factors combined to insure the success of the overall resistance movement. The Seri Thai in the United States had gained support from official agencies and OSS agents were poised to infiltrate Thailand. The Seri Thai in England had gained government sponsorship and had sent intelligence teams to India. The resistance movement inside Thailand was engaged in recruiting a wider cadre base and had successfully sent representatives to southern China.

At the same time, anti-Japanese elements within the Phibun government had conducted meetings with Allied representatives without the knowledge of either the resistance movement in Thailand or the Japanese. As a result of the meetings in Chungking, the Allies had learned of the existence of the resistance movement in

Thailand. They finalized their plans to assist that movement with arms, men, and materiel. By 1944 the foundations for a successful resistance operation had been laid. With initial plans made and infiltration operations ready, the time was close for a physical reunion between Pridi's Phai Nai Prathet and the Allies' Phai Nok Prathet resistance movements.

CHAPTER FOUR

INFILTRATION INTO THAILAND, 1943–1944

INFILTRATION OF THAI AGENTS FROM CHINA

The OSS team of Thai agents and their American sponsors in south China suffered from inactivity, frustration, and lack of information from the time of their arrival, eager to continue operations into Thailand. Nicol Smith, determined to remove the agent team from the political constraints of Chungking, transferred the OSS unit to Kunming in November 1943. Because of Chinese delaying tactics, however, no operations were allowed until 1944. Although unhappy with Chinese politics, Thai agents were encouraged by the news brought by Chamkat, Sa-nguan, and Daeng from Thailand. They were anxious to return to Thailand. They remained in Kunming while they searched for horses to support a move to the frontier for infiltration operations. General Claire Chennault made possible the final move to the forward base at Szemao earlier than expected when he personally provided the aircraft needed to move the men and their equipment. The horses left Kunming on 4 January 1944, while the rest of the unit flew to Szemao on 15 January.[1]

Upon arrival at Szemao the men erected powerful radio transmitters and receivers able to communicate with Bangkok, Chungking, Calcutta, and Kandy. During this period they also conducted final operation planning with the Chinese and developed tentative infiltration routes through southern China and Laos into northern Thailand. General Tai Li agreed to provide guides for the

Thai infiltration teams, but it soon became apparent that this "assistance" was another means to delay and obstruct the Thai teams. The first infiltration into Thailand started on 19 February 1944. Colonel Khap led the first group of Thai agents to a departure point at Cheli (now called Chinghung), a small town in the isolated frontier region of China's Yunnan province. According to plans painstakingly coordinated with Tai Li, Chinese guides and support agents would assist the Thai to infiltrate into Thailand. The first five Thai agents were organized in three teams. Karawek Siwichan and Somphong Sanlayaphong made up one team, while Karun Kengradomying and Ian Khamphanon made up a second team. Phon Intharathat was to operate alone.

The agents' missions varied in details, but in essence they were to organize an infiltration route to central Thailand and to establish contact with the Thai underground. Karawek and Somphong were to reconnoiter the northern border area of Thailand. Phon was to build a courier route from Laos to Uttaradit and to act as an escort and supply contact for future teams. Karun's mission was to establish himself in his home town of Uttaradit, and Ian was to do the same in his home town of Lampang.[2]

Each man carried a variety of equipment and currencies. Disguised as itinerant merchants, the men had no difficulty traveling to Cheli. Once there, however, they ran into interminable delays while the Chinese stalled their departure. Finally Somphong and Karawek left without the promised Chinese guides. They moved via Phong Saly in northern Laos and then southeast along the Mekong River to the Thai border. Tragically, they were captured by unsympathetic Thai police at Chiang Saen (Chiang Rai province). Details on what happened are sketchy but apparently their captors killed the two agents and stole their supply of gold and silver.[3]

Phon Intharathat learned of the death of the two agents through the Chinese intelligence system while waiting in Cheli for a guide. He radioed the news to Szemao, where the other agents received the news with shock and anger. The Thai police involved in the incident were unable to hide the fact that they had detained two Thai agents attempting to infiltrate the country. As a result the Japanese learned that radio-equipped agents were entering Thailand. However, the same news also reached the Thai underground. Police General Adun immediately alerted his Santiban. (This was an agency similar to the U.S. Federal Bureau of Investigation and often translated into English as the Criminal Investigation Department.) He instructed Santiban personnel to make every possible effort to assist infiltrators to evade Japanese patrols and to bring them to Bangkok.

In the meantime, Karun and Ian also entered Thailand. When they reached Phrae province, Santiban officers responding to General Adun's orders "captured" the two men and took them to Bangkok without the knowledge of the Japanese.[4] Phon waited at Cheli until the middle of May without receiving the promised Chinese aid. He then returned to Szemao to seek assistance from Smith and M.L. Khap. Phon later returned to Cheli and infiltrated Thailand during the late spring. He was in Phitsanulok carrying out his mission before being "captured." Phon had come under suspicion and felt it safer to avoid the Japanese in this way.[5]

Careful compartmentation of the missions of the three teams kept them separate from each other; none of the three teams knew of the identification or activities of the others. Aside from Phon's report of the deaths of Karawek and Somphong, no information reached Smith and Colonel Khap on the fate of the infiltrators. It was not until the summer of 1944 that the OSS received definite information from the Bangkok-based underground about the safe arrival and activities of Karun, Ian, and Phon.

After sending the first group of five agents to Cheli, Smith and Colonel Khap had the good fortune to meet Father Jean Tong, a Chinese priest who was a political advisor to General Lu of the Ninety-third Division. Father Tong spoke nine languages. His travels in the Chinese border area provided him with detailed knowledge of the region and its peoples. In view of the delays being encountered with Tai Li's intelligence apparatus, Smith asked Father Tong if he would be willing to guide a group of agents to the Thai border in return for funds to build a small church. Father Tong agreed. A second infiltration group, consisting of Bunyen Sasiran, Pao Kham-urai, Phisut Suthat, and Sawat Chiaosakun, made plans to enter Thailand.

The second group, again posing as itinerant merchants, left Cheli in late April 1944. Father Tong planned to cross a narrow neck of Burmese territory that knifed between Laos and China, but heavy Japanese patrol activity and security operations in Burma prevented their crossing. Instead, the party walked some 350 miles through Yunnan, Laos (via Muong Sing), and on to Thailand. The men journeyed through the heart of the monsoon season, lost most of their food and equipment, and suffered repeated attacks of malaria. It took them eighty-seven days to reach Thailand. Soon after Father Tong left the party at the Thai border, the four agents were detected and "captured" by the Santiban. Since Karun and Ian had told General Adun that more Thai agents would be entering Thailand from China, General Adun had alerted his forces to be watching for them.[6]

The four men of the Father Tong party were unable to reach Szemao by radio. Smith and Colonel Khap had no idea whether or not the group had been successful. Finally Father Tong's report that he had seen them safely to the Thai border provided some solace to those at Szemao. After four months of waiting and speculation, the OSS knew only that two of their agents had been killed near Chiang Saen. No one knew the fate of the other seven men. Certainly those in China did not know that the seven agents had been successful in establishing contact with resistance elements in Thailand.

THAI AGENTS INFILTRATE THAILAND FROM INDIA

British intelligence plans for infiltration of their White Elephant agents into Thailand were underway at the same time that the OSS was sending men from China into Thailand. The meetings between Major Arun and Thai representatives in Chungking had speeded up SOE/Force 136 plans to launch their agents from India. Major Arun's trip to China, which the British dubbed Operation Pritchard, included the attempt to communicate with the Thai underground with microfilm (see chapter 3). The submarine that kept the unsuccessful rendezvous off the Thai coast included three of the White Elephants—Puay Ungphakon, Samran Wannaphruek, and Prathan Premkamon. Unfortunately, the failure of that rendezvous delayed infiltration by the three men. They returned to India to wait for another chance.[7]

In early 1944 the White Elephants began to prepare for final deployment. They received mountain training and airborne instruction as well as survival training. British intelligence considered four methods of infiltration. They discarded an overland route from China because of the distances and time involved and increased Japanese patrol activity. Submarine infiltration was attractive because the agents could be landed close to their destination. However, this method was initially discarded as an unacceptable risk of a valuable ship and crew and because of the lack of shore reception parties to meet the agents. Air landing by Catalina flying boats was considered but discarded for the same reasons. Air drop was the fourth and only remaining feasible method.[8] As it turned out this flying boat method of infiltration was so successful that the Catalina was routinely used to pick up and deliver Thai passengers after the underground had established a network of agents to meet the aircraft.

There was a very real risk of a parachute drop of agents without a reception party on the ground (a "blind drop"). The British minimized the dangers because of the advantages of security and knowledge of the area on the part of the Thai agents. Even so, Force 136 planners had difficulty in drawing up a list of suitable drop zones because of the scarcity and unreliability of their maps. Photographic reconnaissance missions by the Royal Air Force provided more details for the initial missions. The difficulties in obtaining sufficient quantities of reliable maps led to a high priority requirement for better maps and current cartographic data.

Force 136 selected for its first parachute landing mission an area in the mountainous region west of the central Thai plain. British planners gave the operation the code name Operation Appreciation and the two teams of Thai agents became Appreciation I and Appreciation II. Team I included Puay Ungphakon, Prathan Premkamon, and Prem Buri. Team II consisted of Samran Wannaphruek, Rachit Buri, and Thana Potsayanon.[9]

Puay's Appreciation I mission left Calcutta in late February 1944. The men parachuted safely into western Thailand, although they missed the assigned drop by over 25 kilometers. Soon after landing, the three men were spotted by a group of woodcutters who reported them to local officials. Puay managed to avoid the subsequent search effort for three days but was finally apprehended in Wattasing district, Chainat province. Prem and Prathan evaded capture for several more days but were caught while eating in a small restaurant in adjacent Uthai Thani province.[10] The three men were captured by civilians who were not aware of the existence of the underground. Fortunately the agents were turned over to the local Santiban and taken to their headquarters in Bangkok. General Adun's "prison" was becoming crowded with Allied-sponsored agents-in-residence!

Force 136, although worried about the lack of radio contact from Appreciation I, went ahead with the launching of Appreciation II. This team landed according to plan, but they were apprehended by the same group of local villagers and officials. All were taken to the Santiban headquarters.[11]

Thai public radio broadcasted news of the capture of "airborne spies." Force 136 monitored these broadcasts and thus learned that their two teams had reached Bangkok safely.[12] From April to July 1944 this news was the only word that any of the Allied intelligence agencies received of their infiltration operations. Neither the OSS agents nor the Force 136 agents were able to contact their respective headquarters. The Americans and British mistakenly believed that the operations had failed.

THE RECEPTION OF ALLIED AGENTS BY THAI POLICE

Actually the British and American infiltrations had succeeded. The disorganized Thai underground was elated to establish contact with the Thai agents, although at first it was only a one-way contact. Puay and Malai are both vague in their books in pinpointing the exact date of infiltration. Malai and Smith indicate that the American efforts began in February 1944, while the British efforts, as reported by Puay and Gilchrist, refer to April 1944. It appears that the OSS infiltration started the first overland operations, although Force 136 attempted the first infiltration (i.e. the

December 1943 submarine mission). The ill-fated Karawek-Somphong mission was the first group to reach Thailand. The dates of the Karun-Ian, Father Tong, and Appreciation I and II missions are more difficult to determine. These four groups all entered close together in April 1944.

The key underground installation, as far as the Allied agents were concerned, was General Adun's Santiban headquarters in Bangkok. By the end of April 1944, Adun had under his control all six members of Appreciation I and II, the survivors of the first OSS overland infiltration (Karun and Ian), and Phon. The agents learned that they were in safe hands only after reaching Bangkok; some of their captors were not members of the underground. Only when General Adun interviewed the captured agents and revealed his underground affiliation did the Thai agents realize they were in safe hands and had succeeded in locating the underground movement in Thailand.

Although Thanpuying La-iat Phibunsongkhram's account asserts that Phibun knew of the arrival of the agents in Bangkok, there is no evidence that any of Phibun's other confidantes had knowledge of the Thai agents at the Santiban headquarters. An examination of several Thai sources indicates that it was at this point, marked by the arrival of almost a dozen Allied-sponsored agents, that Adun and Pridi became major partners in the resistance movement. Apparently Adun told Pridi of the arrival of the agents.

The Japanese had already learned through their intelligence network that Thai agents were infiltrating Thailand. They made repeated requests to the Thai police that they be allowed to interrogate them. The agreement between Thailand and Japan concerning custody of captured prisoners worked to the advantage of the resistance movement. At no time did any Allied agent come under unilateral Japanese control, although Japanese officials were permitted to "interview" several of them in the presence of Thai police.[13]

During the spring and summer of 1944 the number of agents at Santiban increased. In late April two more White Elephants, Sawat Sisuk and Chunkheng Rinthakun, were parachuted into central Thailand. Adun's men brought them to Bangkok. By July, Santiban

Map 2: Thai Agent Infiltration Routes, Spring 1944

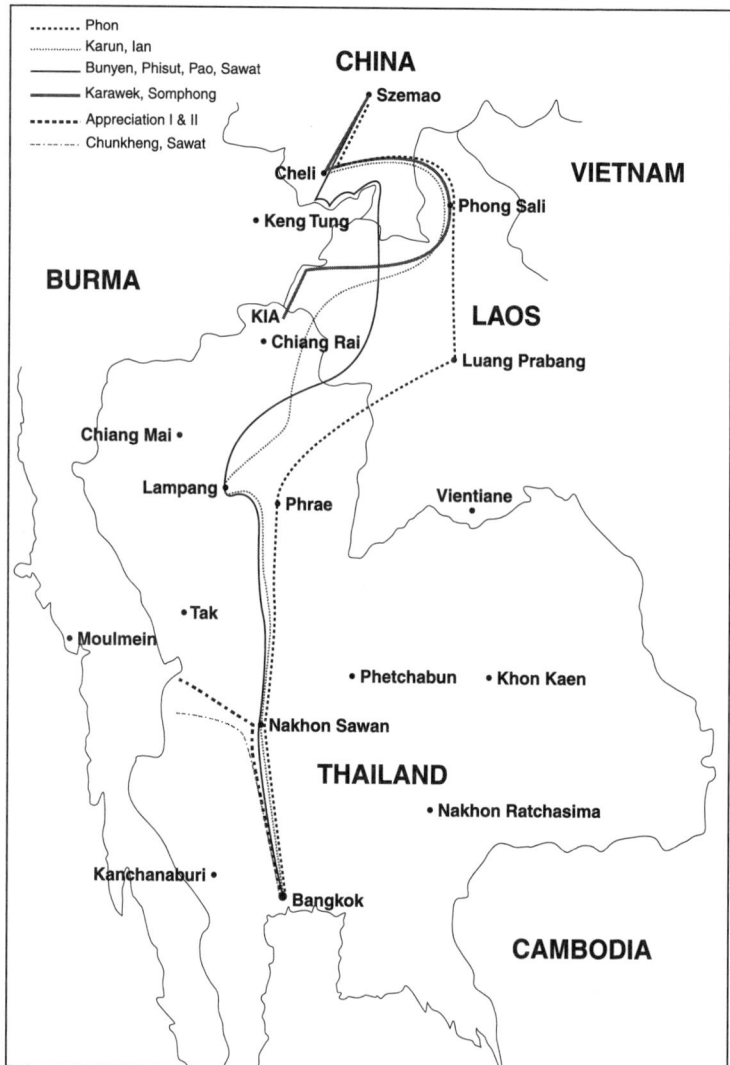

.... Phon
.... Karun, Ian
———— Bunyen, Phisut, Pao, Sawat
———— Karawek, Somphong
- - - - - Appreciation I & II
—··—··— Chunkheng, Sawat

CHINA

Szemao

VIETNAM

Cheli

Keng Tung

Phong Sali

BURMA

KIA

Chiang Rai

LAOS

Luang Prabang

Chiang Mai •

Lampang

Phrae

Vientiane
•

• Tak

• Moulmein

• Phetchabun   • Khon Kaen

Nakhon Sawan

THAILAND

• Nakhon Ratchasima

Kanchanaburi •

Bangkok

CAMBODIA

officers also had escorted the American-sponsored Father Tong party to Bangkok. This brought the total number of Allied agents in Bangkok to fifteen: seven OSS agents and eight White Elephants. In addition, Puay mentioned that seven Sino-Thai infiltrated by submarine were also apprehended and taken to Santiban headquarters.[14] It is possible that these men, of whom little information is available, were part of the Force 136 "Reds" mentioned in chapter 3. The infiltration locations of the several groups of agents reaching Thailand during the spring of 1944 are shown in map 2.

ESTABLISHMENT OF COMMUNICATIONS BETWEEN BANGKOK AND THE ALLIES

Although several parties of Allied agents reached Thailand in the spring of 1944, none was able to contact their headquarters with the radio equipment brought with them. With the concentration of agents in Bangkok, all parties began coordinated efforts to adapt the police communications gear so the agents could contact China and India. While attempts continued to achieve radio communication, Puay prepared a lengthy report for Force 136 headquarters. In an unknown manner this report, inserted into the Chinese intelligence net in Bangkok, made its way to Kunming via Tai Li's communications system. It was relayed to India where the information reached Force 136 in August 1944. Puay reported that the six Appreciation I and II agents were safe in Bangkok but were unable to communicate by radio. He also reported the arrival of "some" OSS agents. This vague report was the first information the intelligence agencies received about their infiltration efforts.

Puay finally made radio contact with Force 136 in August, using equipment that belonged to the Thai Department of Propaganda.[15] He passed a wealth of information to Force 136. Among other items, he identified Pridi as the chief of the Thai resistance movement and General Adun as a major underground figure. He also described the unusual circumstances of the agents in Bangkok, who were prisoners by day but free by night to attempt radio transmissions and to liase with Thai resistance leaders.

Force 136 relayed the information received from Puay to the OSS, but the news did not reach Szemao. OSS headquarters was skeptical of the accuracy of Puay's reports. Some American intelligence officers believed that the Thai were permitting Allied agents to report only material selected by the Thai government. Throughout the war, OSS remained suspicious of General Adun's loyalties and degree of cooperation with the resistance movement.

Because of their suspicion that previous agent teams had been compromised, OSS decided to infiltrate another agent team into Thailand, with orders to report only to Pridi and to avoid being lodged in the Santiban prison. This mission was controlled from India; the OSS group at Szemao was not told of the plans.

The agents chosen for the mission, Bunmak Thetsabut and Wimon Wiriyawit, were members of the original Free Thai Army but they had not been members of the group that sailed with Nicol Smith. After completing training in the United States they traveled with a second group of OSS-trained agents for intelligence duties in Ceylon and India. Bunmak and Wimon were first taken toward the Thai coast by submarine but bad weather prevented them from landing and the mission was aborted.[16] This failure led the OSS to return to the more familiar system of parachute drops.

The two men parachuted into Phrae province on 9 September 1944. They attempted to locate two underground cadre members whose names had been given to American authorities by Sa-nguan Tularak. Though separated, they used their wits and both ended up traveling safely to Bangkok. They went into police custody, as had other agents, and then were allowed to meet with leaders of the resistance.[17]

Bunmak and Wimon told Pridi of the American offer to assist, if acceptable, the Thai resistance movement with men, equipment, and training. They also told Pridi that the State Department was sympathetic to their efforts and political goals.[18] Pridi was elated at such good news. American support would enable him to provide arms to his planned guerrilla movement. Although admittedly a sketchy "promise," delivered in an indirect manner, the possibility of tangible American support was welcome. In all probability this report had more to do with the expansion of the resistance movement inside Thailand than any other single event.

Wimon, who had a remarkable degree of movement—always with a police escort—was disappointed at the lack of development in the resistance organization inside Thailand. In a private meeting with General Adun he attempted to persuade the police chief to align himself formally with Pridi's resistance movement. Wimon also briefed Direk on the political situation outside Thailand, and urged internal cooperation and coordination between all anti-Japanese elements in Thailand.[19] This meeting, on 22 September 1944, was extremely important in bringing together the powerful leaders of the police and the civilian government aligned with Pridi.

Back in the U.S., recruitment of Thai youths by the Thai legation into the OSS program was so successful that a second group of fifteen Thai officers was trained. They left for Asia in April 1944. Another three Thai applied directly to the OSS, and infiltration of OSS agents continued as well.[20] In November three more men dropped by parachute onto the rugged mountains of Chiang Mai province. Unfortunately the operation was so insecure—the aircraft reportedly circled directly over the city of Chiang Mai to get its bearings—that the Japanese were tipped off. The three men parachuted safely into the mountains and collected most of their equipment. General Adun's police found the three agents— Chaloem, Udomsak, and Sit—and moved them successfully to Bangkok.[21] But because the Japanese knew all about the landing they demanded custody of the agents. As a compromise the three were placed in a Thai-managed prisoner-of-war camp but not before OSS in Szemao was notified of what had transpired.[22]

In the meantime the British were planning an immediate expansion of their own efforts to infiltrate Thailand. Encouraged by radio contact with the White Elephants, Force 136 planned to introduce additional agent teams into Thailand. Puay recommended that all future parachute drops of agents and equipment be made in coordination with reception teams on the ground, which would be provided by the expanding Thai resistance movement. He recommended that sea infiltrations should be made only when shore reception parties could be provided. Force 136 followed these recommendations, with a few exceptions, for the rest of the war. The next British mission was launched in early September 1944. Code-named Operation Brillig, the plan called for parachuting two agents into a landing area near the coastal town of Hua Hin, in Prachuap Khiri Khan province on the Kra Isthmus. The two agents, Krit Totsayanon and Prasoet Pathummanon, landed safely on 6 September 1944. A small reception party met them and arranged their onward travel to Bangkok by Thai Customs Service patrol boat. They too met with Pridi and delivered an offer of material assistance from Lord Louis Mountbatten, commander in chief of the Southeast Asia Command (SEAC) in Ceylon. It contained much the same offers of support as did the American message delivered by Bunmak and Wimon.[23]

The two parachute drops by the American and British intelligence agencies were not coordinated. The OSS considered their mission to Pridi so sensitive that they did not inform Force 136. At the same time Force 136, energized by the apparent success of their infiltration and communications to Bangkok, did not tell the Americans of their activities. As a result, the two parachute operations took place within three days of each other, at opposite ends of the country. The two teams carried virtually identical offers of support to the Thai resistance. This was a typical example of the lack of cooperation and coordination in Allied intelligence operations.

September 1944 was the most active month for the Thai resistance movement since its formation. Within days of each other the United States and England both gave firm offers of materiel and personnel support. The resistance succeeded in establishing effective communications with India using their own radios. Furthermore, the resistance demonstrated their reaction capabilities and internal coordination by the efficient manner in which they advised, assisted, and coordinated the Krit-Prasoet operation at Hua Hin.

The OSS finally achieved communications between Bangkok and Szemao on 5 October 1944, when Pao contacted them after months of attempting to communicate using a variety of Thai police department radios. He reported essentially the same information to Szemao as Puay had sent to India. He confirmed the deaths of

Karawek and Somphong, the safe arrival in Bangkok of the other seven agents, and identified Pridi as leader of the resistance.[24] Although the OSS headquarters and Force 136 already had this information, it was news to Smith and M.L. Khap. There is no explanation why the OSS agents took so much longer to contact their headquarters than the Force 136 agents did. It is possible that the radio equipment was responsible. The OSS maintained a constant radio watch in Szemao but had to wait from April until October to hear from their agents. The establishment of the OSS radio link completed the required network in the Allied intelligence communications system with Thailand. Later the use of more powerful equipment would make communications routine between Bangkok, China, India, and Ceylon. The expansion of the internal communications net within Thailand also improved underground operations. This communications system is diagrammed in figure 1.

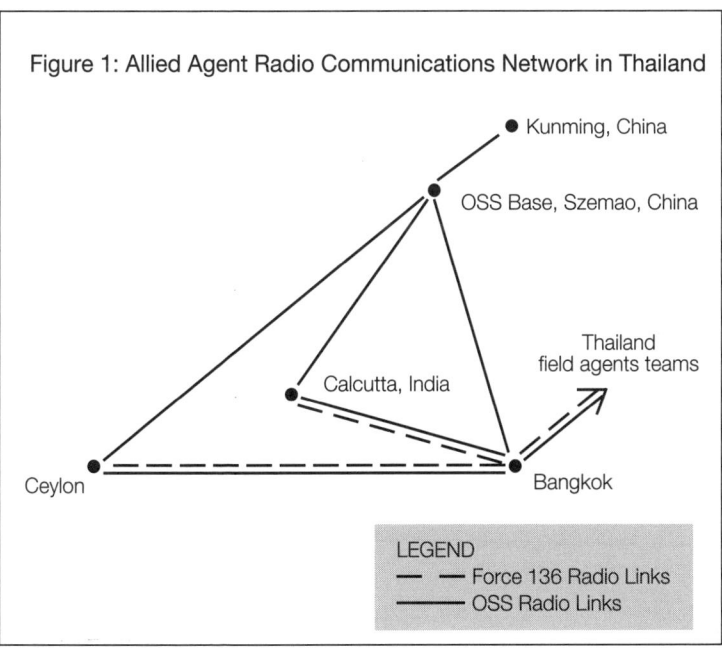

Figure 1: Allied Agent Radio Communications Network in Thailand

Kunming, China

OSS Base, Szemao, China

Calcutta, India

Thailand field agents teams

Ceylon

Bangkok

LEGEND
— — Force 136 Radio Links
—— OSS Radio Links

The Allies, with the establishment of reliable and rapid communications, began more effective operations to gather information on the political and military situation inside Thailand. They also had learned the need for better coordination after the September 1944 operations. By late 1944 inter-service coordination was much improved and contributed to the effectiveness of Allied intelligence-gathering operations. The three items of greatest concern to OSS were information on military targets for air force bombing missions and associated twenty-four-hour weather data, all available information on Japanese troop movements into Burma and Malaya, and the locations of Allied prisoner-of-war camps. The Americans also needed political information. OSS tasked agents to gather information on the Thai government's views and those of the resistance movement, on such issues as French rule in Indochina and British rule in Malaya, as well as Thai attitudes toward the Allies.[25] Force 136 set similar requirements on their agents, with emphasis on the Thai-Burma railroad and its associated prisoner-of-war camps.[26]

INFILTRATION OF SINO-THAI AGENTS INTO THAILAND

The role of Sino-Thai agents in Thai resistance operations is unclear. Several agencies previously mentioned in this book actively used Chinese and Sino-Thai agents. General Tai Li had the largest network, but his operations were secret. In all probability the scope of such operations was known only by Tai Li, certainly not by other Allied intelligence agencies. The OSS discovered early in the war that Tai Li had a well-established intelligence network that reached into Thailand, Burma, and Indochina. Its role in carrying Puay Ungphakon's written report to British intelligence in India showed that it was a competent and capable organization. Unfortunately, there are virtually no reports available in English that discuss the history and activities of Tai Li's network and its contributions to the war effort in Southeast Asia.

The OSS estimated that as many as fifteen hundred Sino-Thai left Thailand for China to help the Allied war effort. Tai Li took control of them for military training and political indoctrination.[27]

The Japanese made brief references to officers of the "War Direction Bureau." They used the term "Blue Shirt Society" to refer to Chinese agents infiltrated by any manner into Thailand. The Japanese believed that those who succeeded in reaching Thailand went to Bangkok and, disguised as Chinese merchants, blended into the population. Apparently they conducted liaison with, but were not an integral part of, Pridi's resistance movement.[28]

Gilchrist briefly mentions the Sino-Thai "Red" and "Blue" agents recruited by SOE in China and trained for operations into Thailand. Operation Billow was a Force 136 effort in May 1944 to infiltrate a four-man team of "Reds" into Thailand. Led by Captain Ngit Yin Kok, they were landed by Catalina flying boat off the coast of southern Thailand and safely reached the shore. They never established radio contact with Force 136. Later word reached Ceylon that the four had either been killed or captured.[29] The infiltration locations for the "Reds," as well as the parachuted OSS and SOE agent teams, are shown in map 3.

Several Thai sources mention hearing of or seeing Chinese agents in various prisons inside Thailand, but no confirming documentation has been found. Both the OSS and Force 136 made use of Sino-Thai agents in their operations into Thailand, but no account of such operations could be located. It is one of the least-known aspects of World War II intelligence operations in Thailand.

INTELLIGENCE GATHERING IN THAILAND

The key to timely intelligence gathering activity in Thailand was successful communication with Allied intelligence agencies. Secure communications meant that the Thai agents could quickly pass information to their sponsors, almost as soon as the Thai obtained the information. Initially all radio communications in Bangkok were handled inside the Santiban headquarters building. Later, as the Allied presence in Bangkok expanded, the intelligence support structure manned additional stations in other locations.

There were several benefits in using the Santiban building. First, the Thai police radio station was there. Japanese radio direction-

Map 3: Thai Agent Infiltration Locations, Summer/Fall 1944

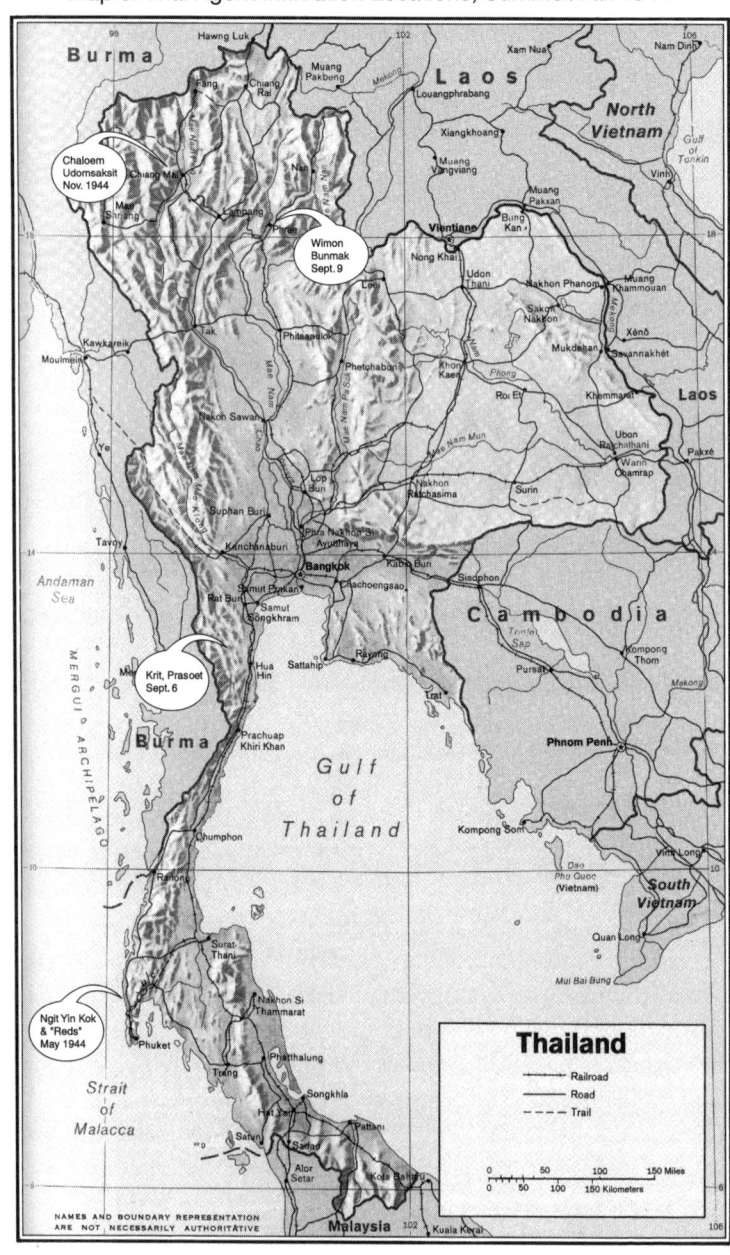

finding efforts had little effect on the agent communications system because such efforts were diverted by legitimate police communications. Second, agents were almost totally secure in moving about the building. Third, Thai members of the underground had plausible reasons to visit: ordinary citizens came daily to the building. Fourth, the building provided excellent cover for movement of Thai agent "prisoners" to meet with underground cadres from other areas of the city.

Radio operations in Thailand were standardized. Both Force 136 and the OSS established transmission schedules and levied information requirements on their agents. Police Captain Phayom Chantarakha, a Seri Thai confidante of both Pridi and Adun, acted as the primary liaison officer for the agents. Professor Wichit Lulitanon, another Pridi associate, also was a liaison officer and escort for the agents. He often took agents to meetings with Pridi in his automobile.[30]

The Thai agents quickly formed an efficient system of operations. They informed the underground of information requirements and then acted as the radio relay link to the Allies.

Initially the Thai agents were not required to gather intelligence.[31] During their early period in Thailand the agents were confined to the Santiban building except for visits to Pridi, so they could not gather intelligence. During that time (mid 1944) the resistance movement had not yet expanded into the provinces in sufficient numbers to support Thai agents' intelligence collection activities. Until the resistance was able to expand, the Thai agents were totally dependent on the Thai resistance membership for intelligence collection. Later several of the agents were assigned to organize intelligence nets in other areas of Thailand.

The first radioed intelligence reached the OSS on 7 October 1944. Pao Kham-urai relayed a list of potential bombing targets to Szemao, along with a lengthy report on Japanese military organization, the location of units, and projected weather data. The information was taken from the accumulated files of the underground.[32] The intelligence collection initiated by Pridi in 1942 had finally reached the Allies.

These reports were the beginning of a flood of raw, unevaluated information from Thailand to the Allies. This raw information was useful for it included lists of military targets for bombing raids and reports on the results of Allied air raids. Virtually every movement of Japanese troop units was reported to the Allies. Through contact with the Thai embassy in Tokyo, the underground received and passed to the agents reports of damage from air raids over Japan, as well as information on the internal political and military situation.[33] The first U.S. B-29 raid in history was based on information collected by Thais in Japan, passed to the resistance leadership in Bangkok, and reported by the Thai agents to the OSS.

Probably the single most valuable man during this phase of intelligence dependence on the resistance movement was LTC Samroeng Nettrayon. He was a Thai intelligence officer in Bangkok who served as the primary liaison officer between the Thai Supreme Command and the Japanese army headquarters. His ability to obtain top-level information from the Japanese high command in Thailand was extremely helpful to Allied intelligence. He provided detailed information on planned Japanese troop movements that enabled the Allies to locate and bomb troop trains. LTC Samroeng also reported on Japanese analysis of Allied military intentions that was valuable in planning Allied military operations throughout Southeast Asia.[34]

While the basic type of information collected by the resistance movement was helpful to the Allied cause, Allied intelligence agencies found shortcomings in its accuracy. Furthermore, there was no direction or management of the intelligence gathering operation; information was obtained on the basis of what was easily available. This left gaps in intelligence knowledge. Both the OSS and the SOE found that the information lacked detail or omitted important facts. Western intelligence agencies concluded that the Thai officials were willing and able to assist, but lacked training in information collection, evaluation, and reporting.

To overcome these problems OSS decided to send American intelligence officers into Thailand to train the Thais in the details of intelligence collection.[35] The British cited problems of imprecise locational reporting, poor transliteration of Thai place names, and lack of needed details.[36] A retired American military intelligence officer reviewed over eighty randomly selected reports produced by the OSS on the basis of information sent from Bangkok. He determined that the primary deficiencies in the reporting were a lack of distances and dimensions on sketches, frequent omission of identifiable points of reference, and an overall lack of the small details that would be overlooked by untrained intelligence collectors but which were vital for proper analysis and planning. For example, one report was a beautifully drawn sketch of a Japanese military compound, complete with the location and identification of all troop billets and motor vehicles. The reporter neglected, however, to give the location of the compound.[37] Because of such omissions, valuable potential military bombing targets could not be exploited by the Allies.

American and British intelligence agencies proposed, in separate messages to Pridi, that Allied instructors be sent to train Thai resistance members in intelligence collection, guerrilla operations, and secret communications systems. Pridi readily agreed to the requests; in fact, he prepared a written plan for locating the training facilities.

Pridi entrusted Thawin Udon, a close friend from Phrae province, to hand-carry his plan to the Allies. Karun Kengradomying, one of the first OSS infiltrators, escorted Thawin to the OSS camp in Szemao, China. They became the first OSS personnel to negotiate successfully the return trip from Thailand to China. The two Thais arrived at Szemao on 20 November 1944 then flew to Kunming. At first the Chinese refused to allow OSS officers to debrief Thawin. But Karun knew enough of Pridi's plan to brief Smith and M.L. Khap.

Smith thought the plan of sufficient importance to send Karun and Chamrat Follett, the ranking Thai agent in Colonel Khap's absence, to the United States to brief American intelligence personnel. While some changes were made in Pridi's proposal, the plan formed the basis for later provision of men, weapons, equipment, and training to the Thai resistance.[38] Both Chamrat and Karun rejoined the OSS effort in Ceylon after their mission to Washington, D.C.

THE IMPORTANCE OF THE ALLIED INFILTRATION
EFFORTS

By November 1944, contacts between the Allies, their agents in Thailand, and with the Thai underground were in regular operation. Pridi, who by then had received his famous code name, "Ruth," Adun (code named Betty), and Captain Prayun (Patsy) successfully transmitted a report of their requirements to the Allies. Both the United States and England were prepared to supply the Thai resistance movement with the necessary means to expand its strength and fighting capability. This assistance was the result of information obtained from the resistance leadership and transmitted to the Allies by the agents who had successfully infiltrated Bangkok.

The Allies were surprised at the extent of Pridi's resistance movement and the base it provided for expansion of intelligence collection and guerrilla operations. From November 1944 until the Japanese surrender some ten months later, Allied operations into and inside Thailand became almost routine. The Allies' determination to support the resistance movement provided the basis for expansion of that movement to include most of Thailand. This could not have occurred without the on-the-spot evaluation of Thai agents sent to Bangkok by the OSS and the SOE.

Equally important, the Allied intelligence agencies had finally discovered that they could cooperate in many aspects of operations into Thailand. Organizational rivalries never disappeared, but for all intents and purposes the last year of the war saw great improvements in inter-service cooperation in intelligence activities. As 1944 drew to a close the two organizations were prepared to act in cooperation with each other to enhance their mutual requirements and together to support the Thai resistance movement.

Inside the resistance movement profound changes were taking place. The painstaking process to recruit trustworthy members and to expand the scope and coverage of the resistance movement had resulted in a cohesive, powerful resistance movement with almost complete political control over the Thai government as well. It is necessary to view this period of expansion and consolidation of power in the overall context of events taking place inside Thailand as well as outside the country but with immediate impact on its future. The next chapter examines the process by which the resistance movement acquired strength and numbers, and engaged in active resistance against the Japanese.

CHAPTER FIVE

BUILDING THE RESISTANCE BASE, 1942–1945

EXPANSION OF THE RESISTANCE ORGANIZATION

The early efforts of the Thai resistance movement to form an effective base to organize anti-Japanese political and military activities were covered in the earlier chapters. To recapitulate, Pridi recruited civilian friends into an inner circle of leadership, while the police and military factions conducted independent measures to resist the Japanese. Phibun planned contacts with the Chinese and eventually lost his position as prime minister in a political confrontation with liberal Thai leaders. The Thais began, during this same period, to take advantage of opportunities to harass the enemy. Consolidation of these many variant efforts came late in the war. Coordinated resistance did not begin until Phibun resigned and Khuang Aphaiwong became prime minister in August 1944.

Expansion of the resistance movement was slow but steady. Recruits came from all walks of life, but those closest to Pridi were long-time friends and associates. The pattern of expansion was sporadic. When Pridi recruited a new member of the underground he expanded the resistance movement's area of influence into the area in which the new member resided. The resistance leadership attempted to locate new members in all areas of the country, but gaps in resistance influence and thus in geographical coverage did result. Generally speaking, the resistance movement was strong in those areas where Pridi had a loyal personal following, the population had particular cause to dislike the Japanese, or local figures were able to form offshoots of the central resistance effort.

Early recruits to the resistance leadership who had personal power centers outside of Bangkok included National Assemblymen Phueng Sichan (Uttaradit), Thong Kanthatham (Phrae), and Chaowong Saensiriphan (Phrae).[1] Other early leaders were Governor Udom Bunyaprakop (Khon Kaen) who was the chief of resistance units that were formed in Khon Kaen and Loei provinces,[2] Chamlong Daorueang (Maha Sarakham), and Thong-in Phuriphat (Ubon Ratchathani). Thawin Udon apparently was in charge of all resistance operations in northern Thailand until his successful trip to China with Karun Kengradomying in November 1944.

One of the most important operational leaders of the underground was Chan Bunnak. He operated from Hua Hin and was in charge of operations in the near south provinces of Prachuap Khiri Khan, Phetchaburi, Ratchaburi, and Chumphon. Chan played a major role in the reception of air drop operations. It was he who met Force 136 agents Prasoet and Krit when they parachuted into Thailand in September 1944. Pridi placed Chan in charge of all underground security measures and his work won him praise from the Allies after the war. He also endeared himself to many of the Thai agents who infiltrated to Bangkok. They frequently used Chan's spacious Bangkok home as their quarters.

Chan attributed the success of the operations under his control to his use of good security practices and reliance only on close friends and relatives in his operations.[3] These practices quickly spread throughout the underground. Many leaders in the resistance formed their own cells from members of their families and close associates in their work or business. The pervasive role of the extended Thai family was essential to the expansion and success of the resistance movement. As the resistance organization spread to all areas of the country, the closeness of family leadership was a common factor in individual organization in the provinces.

By 1944 the underground had succeeded in placing active resistance units in most regions of the country. Units under civilians were established in Kanchanaburi (Khun Phichaimontri) and Prachuap Khiri Khan (Chan Bunnak and Udom Bunyaprakop).

Military officers headed units in the difficult southern provinces of Nakhon Si Thammarat (Major Sawaeng Na Phatthalung) and Surat Thani (Major Sawat Krairoek). The participation of the Thai police Santiban organization was further evidence of a greater level of inter-agency cooperation within the Thai government. Santiban officers headed resistance units in Phang-nga (Captain Prasat Suwanna-sombun), Krabi (Captain Chao Khlaisamrit), and Chumphon (Captain Chaisong Amphunan). Units also were established in Songkhla and Phatthalung provinces. In a significant political alliance, Police Colonel Bunchong Chippensuk formed a small unit in Saiburi in southern Thailand that established contacts with Ta Lee and A Yang, leaders in the Malaya Communist Party involved in anti-Japanese activity inside Malaya.[4]

In the north, large resistance units were formed in many of the mountainous provinces. The Uttaradit unit, with over five thousand men, became the largest one in the north. Other units were formed by Yai Sawichat in Nakhon Sawan; Chaloei Chaithat and Prasit Kikrachinda in Sukhothai; and Arun Sonthet in Tak and Kam-phaeng Phet.[5] See figure 2 for the organization of units throughout the country by 1944.

The influence of Western missionaries and their Thai Christian congregations was of particular importance in forming resistance efforts in the north. While many Western missionaries were forced to flee the Japanese advances, others remained behind. Lucy Starling reports that a physician in Phrae province treated wounded soldiers at a secret resistance base and another physician in Phitsanulok province assisted several Allied airmen to elude capture until they could be spirited to safety.[6] Dr. John Holladay, a missionary who had left Thailand through Burma at the start of the war, later returned in an unusual way. He parachuted into Thailand with the rank of major in the OSS and conducted resistance activities and anti-Japanese propaganda warfare from a medical clinic.[7] By 1945 the underground had well-established units in most areas of the country and were actively recruiting men for guerrilla units.

CONSOLIDATION OF POWER AND EXPANSION OF THE RESISTANCE MOVEMENT

Phibun's resignation as prime minister and his replacement by Khuang Aphaiwong, a member of the resistance leadership, marked a quantum jump in the power and influence of the resistance movement. Pridi moved rapidly to consolidate both his official position as regent and as the leader of the resistance movement. As head of government, Khuang appointed staunch resistance supporters to positions of power in the military and in the civilian departments. Leaders of the resistance were able to move more freely about the country. Many long-time leaders of the resistance did not assume an official position and continued to exercise leadership from the relative anonymity of their private status.

Phibun's resignation marked a major shift in loyalties for the police and military. The leaders of the two most powerful organizations in the country, long personally loyal to Phibun, had been hampered in their support of the resistance by their kinship and patron ties to him. In the summer of 1944 both the police and the

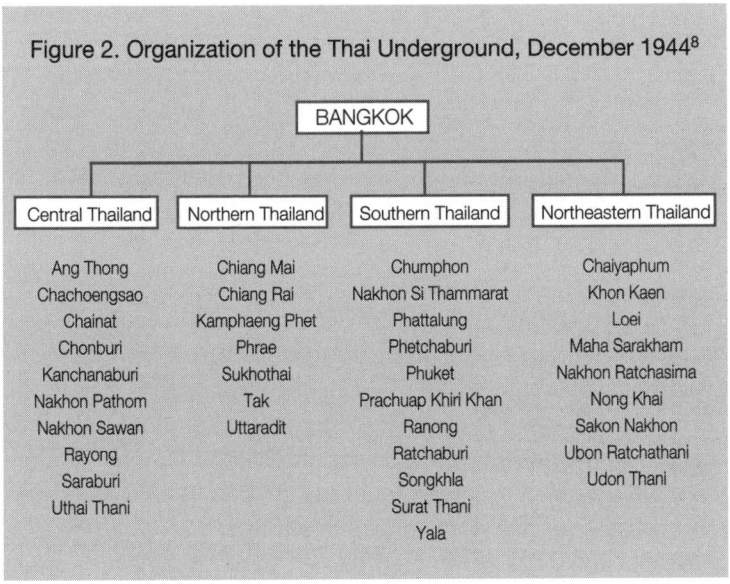

Figure 2. Organization of the Thai Underground, December 1944[8]

BANGKOK			
Central Thailand	Northern Thailand	Southern Thailand	Northeastern Thailand
Ang Thong	Chiang Mai	Chumphon	Chaiyaphum
Chachoengsao	Chiang Rai	Nakhon Si Thammarat	Khon Kaen
Chainat	Kamphaeng Phet	Phattalung	Loei
Chonburi	Phrae	Phetchaburi	Maha Sarakham
Kanchanaburi	Sukhothai	Phuket	Nakhon Ratchasima
Nakhon Pathom	Tak	Prachuap Khiri Khan	Nong Khai
Nakhon Sawan	Uttaradit	Ranong	Sakon Nakhon
Rayong		Ratchaburi	Ubon Ratchathani
Saraburi		Songkhla	Udon Thani
Uthai Thani		Surat Thani	
		Yala	

armed forces chiefs became important members of the leadership echelon of the resistance movement. The resistance movement now had the loyalty of virtually all the members of the military, police, civil service, and the population as a whole. It was inevitable that the resistance's influence expanded rapidly to the provinces and advanced from a small group of leadership cadres to a movement of real strength and potential for paramilitary operations.

No longer did most resistance activities occur without the knowledge of the Thai government. For all intents and purposes the resistance movement became the government. From mid-August 1944 onward, the government's primary concern was to obtain whatever possible benefits were available to assist Thailand in improving its image in the eyes of the Allies. The change of government brought to power, through peaceful and constitutional change, the anti-Japanese oligarchy without incurring undue suspicion or wrath from the Japanese. The official U.S. War Department history of the Office of Strategic Services described the new position of the Thai resistance movement as:

> a patriotic governmental conspiracy . . . not the usual underground groups, but . . . responsible and official heads of a sovereign state, naturally and properly concerned with obtaining for their country the greatest possible benefits at the least cost . . . There was no reason to doubt the anti-Japanese and pro-Allied sentiment of the underground leaders, nor their conviction in the final victory of the Allies, but fundamentally they were motivated less by hatred of the Japanese, or sympathy with Allied war aims, than by the patriotic desire to serve the long-term interests of Siam.[9]

It is a matter of speculation whether or not the Japanese occupation authorities realized the major impact the change of governments brought to the Thai political scene. Certainly the Japanese in Thailand realized the overt political implications of the change. They probably agreed to the ouster of "their man" Phibun for three reasons. First, they could not provide sufficient military force to garrison Thailand while still fighting in Burma and Malaya. Seizure of the Thai government would have brought opposition requiring such a force. Second, the Japanese must have known that Phibun had the interests of his own country at heart rather than those of Japan. He was not so pro-Japanese that his ouster was significant to them. Third, the Japanese intelligence apparatus apparently underestimated the strength and power of the resistance movement. Japan felt sufficiently secure in their formal alliance with Thailand to permit a known foe of Phibun's political views and policies to become prime minister.

The Thai underground moved cautiously after seizing political power. They avoided any precipitous actions that would force the Japanese to take over the government or disarm the Thai armed forces. The result was an outward continuation of the political status quo. The new Thai government would have preferred, but did not dare, to denounce the alliance with Japan. So the Khuang government continued most policies of the Phibun government in its dealings with the Japanese, but provided greater latitude for resistance operations. On the surface, Prime Minister Khuang was the model of a political ally to Japanese leadership. But with him and many of his ministers, also members of the resistance movement, the government was in a position to assist markedly in planning and carrying out the expansion of the resistance.

THE ROLE OF THE THAI ARMED FORCES IN RESISTANCE ACTIVITY

The three branches of the Thai armed forces conducted anti-Japanese activities from the start of the war. Much of the combat strength of the armed forces was dissipated with the assignment of many army personnel to duties in the provinces. However, the staffs of the three military services and their associated field force headquarters had, within their ranks, many men who had been early members of the resistance movement. Initially only a few military officers were members of the inner circle of the underground. Although most leaders of the military services paid lip service to the Japanese, their real loyalties were with the resistance movement. In the first years of the war, however, the three services carried out their anti-Japanese activities independently and were not under the control of the underground leadership.

The most important change in military force loyalty occurred in the army. With the resignation of Phibun, who also served as army Supreme Commander, the Royal Thai Army swung completely behind the resistance movement. For political reasons and to insure harmony with Phibun, Khuang appointed as army commander in chief the aged but much-revered Phot Phahonyothin. Many of the day-to-day command duties and responsibilities were assumed by the deputy commander in chief, General Chit Mansin Sinat-yotharak, who became a member of the X.O. Group. Pridi had the support of the military high command as well as considerable control over its arms and equipment for integration into the total strength of the resistance movement. Elements of the military infrastructure distracted the Japanese or planned for eventual combat with the Japanese forces. In the far north of Thailand Colonel Chalo Inthara-amphon (also known as Phra Apahi Phonla-rop) organized guerrilla units among the minority hill tribes. His son Prayun and he were members of Thawin Udon's party that reached China with Karun Kengradomying in November 1944.[10]

Admiral Sangwon Yuthakit, deputy commander in chief of the Royal Thai Navy, supported the underground in several capacities. He was a member of the X.O. Group and Pridi's closest confidante among the armed forces. Second, he controlled major naval bases in Chonburi and Prachuap Khiri Khan provinces that became useful as training camps for guerrilla forces. Admiral Sangwon also commanded all military police in the Bangkok area. These men provided security and escort duties for the Thai agents, and later for American and British intelligence officers as well.[11] The naval base in Prachuap Khiri Khan served as a pick-up point for agents and equipment parachuted or flown to the Kra Isthmus. Patrol craft from that base, and from Thai Customs Service bases, met all Catalina landings in the Gulf of Thailand. The bases at Prachuap Khiri Khan also served as a contact point for transshipment of men and equipment to and from Bangkok.[12]

The Royal Thai Air Force, with army assistance, prepared several air bases for use by the resistance forces and their Allied sponsors.

Military forces prepared a number of rough landing strips in remote areas of the country for similar use. Early in the war the air force discovered that the Don Mueang Air Base near Bangkok was ideally suited for use by the underground. The physical arrangement of the base was such (and still is today) that the Japanese utilized only one side of it for their operations. They left the other side for the Thai Air Force. Hanger facilities enabled Thai aircraft carrying both Thai and Western agents to taxi directly into the buildings to discharge passengers and cargo in secrecy.

An airstrip of major importance to the resistance movement was located at Phu Khiao, near the border between Chaiyaphum and Khon Kaen provinces. It had the distinct advantages of isolation and suitable landing facilities; the Japanese could not approach by land without giving warning long in advance. A small Royal Thai Air Force contingent manned the field at the start of the war. However, by 1945 the resistance movement had a force of 19 officers and 240 soldiers stationed at Phu Khiao.[13] The resistance also controlled airstrips in Prachuap Khiri Khan province; at Khlong Phai; at Khok-krathiam near Lopburi; and at Phu Kradung in Loei province. Furthermore, by 1945 resistance force guerrillas built rough airstrips at Na Khu (Maha Sarakham province), Na Pong and Pa Pak (Nakhon Phanom province), and in Sakhon Nakhon, Khon Kaen, Tak, Udon Thani, and Ubon Ratchathani provinces.[14]

Planning for active combat operations against the Japanese army involved almost total cooperation of the military services, police, and underground leadership. The leaders in Thailand consolidated ideas and eventually submitted them for approval to Allied headquarters in Ceylon. The proposal was detailed and included specific tasks for all elements of the Thai infrastructure. Planning was made for two contingencies: first, unilateral Thai-only operations, and, second, for participation in support of an Allied offensive into Thailand.[15]

Even before the arrival of Allied support and equipment or formal instructions for subversive operations, elements of the resistance movement engaged in sabotage operations against the Japanese infrastructure. Favorite targets for small scale acts of destruction were petroleum storage facilities and food supplies. On a larger scale, the resistance wrecked so many Japanese troop and store trains that the army had to commit reinforcements to guard the railroads. The spate of activities against Japanese supply trains became so frequent that in 1943 the Japanese command pressured Phibun to discharge the minister of communications—Khuang Aphaiwong. In an ironical twist of history, he later returned to engage the Japanese at a higher level, as prime minister. But in his position as minister of communications, Khuang helped plan many acts of sabotage against the Japanese.[16] After Khuang became prime minister, Duean Bunnak took over direction of sabotage operations.[17]

JAPANESE COUNTERINTELLIGENCE EFFORTS, 1942–1945

There is little information available on the activities of Japanese security organizations in Thailand. Oblique references to the Japanese intelligence apparatus indicate that they were aware of the existence of an underground organization, but did little to counter it. It does not seem likely that the Japanese knew the identities of all of the leadership echelon, for none were arrested for anti-Japanese activity. During the formative years of the resistance its level of activity was so low that it did not present a major target for the Japanese. The Kempeitai spent most of its time gathering intelligence and investigating isolated attacks against Japanese personnel and logistical stores. A senior Thai official later observed that "Japanese intelligence measures . . . were not very efficient."[18] Official Japanese reports agree with this observation. An evaluation prepared after the war stated: "The intelligence network of the Garrison Army was very lax and its counterintelligence failed to root out enemy spies. It was not until after the war that the full scope of the spy activity was known."[19]

The Japanese military forces themselves became concerned about harassment by the Thai population and later by the organized activities of the resistance movement. The Japanese army in Thailand was a large and lucrative target for harassment and sabotage operations. For the first year of occupation in Thailand the Japanese formed small garrisons of constantly changing headquarter elements. Later on, the Japanese established a full-time military garrison in Thailand. On 4 January 1943 the Japanese Siam Garrison Army (SGA), subordinate to the Southern Army, established its headquarters in Bangkok. General Akito Nakamura, who commanded SGA, had the dual missions to maintain the discipline of Japanese armed forces in Thailand and to secure the cooperation of the Thai government.[20]

By December 1943, the Siam Garrison Army had increased its force size to five infantry battalions formed into the Ninth Independent Infantry Brigade, in addition to a variety of combat support and combat service support units. Significantly, one of the support units was the Second Southern Army Kempeitai, whose mission combined the duties of military intelligence with those of a secret police. Since the total strength of the Siam Garrison Army was never less than fifty thousand men, the military opposition confronting the resistance movement was formidable. The organization of the Siam Garrison Army is diagrammed in figure 3.

On 8 December 1944 the SGA was reorganized into the Thirty-ninth Army and also assumed responsibility for a part of southern Burma. This changed its mission from that of a static occupation headquarters to one of a full-line combat army. One month later the Fourth Division arrived in Thailand from Sumatra and deployed in northern Thailand as part of the Thirty-ninth Army. Its strength increased with the assignment of the Sixty-first Regiment to Bangkok, and movement of units from Chiang Mai to Bangkok added to the Japanese military strength in the capital. The last significant increment of Japanese forces arrived in Thailand in May 1945, when the Thirty-seventh Division began movement from Indochina. Although this division was ordered into combat in Malaya, for a variety of reasons it remained in Bangkok until the end of the war.[21]

By mid 1944 resistance activity had become more pronounced and attracted increased attention from Japanese security personnel. Both Puay and Malai described Japanese demands to question Seri Thai agents "captured" by Thai police. The subsequent Kempeitai questioning sessions revealed that the Japanese knew the Allies were infiltrating Thailand but had no idea of their strength. Through judicious guess and estimate the Japanese began piecing together a

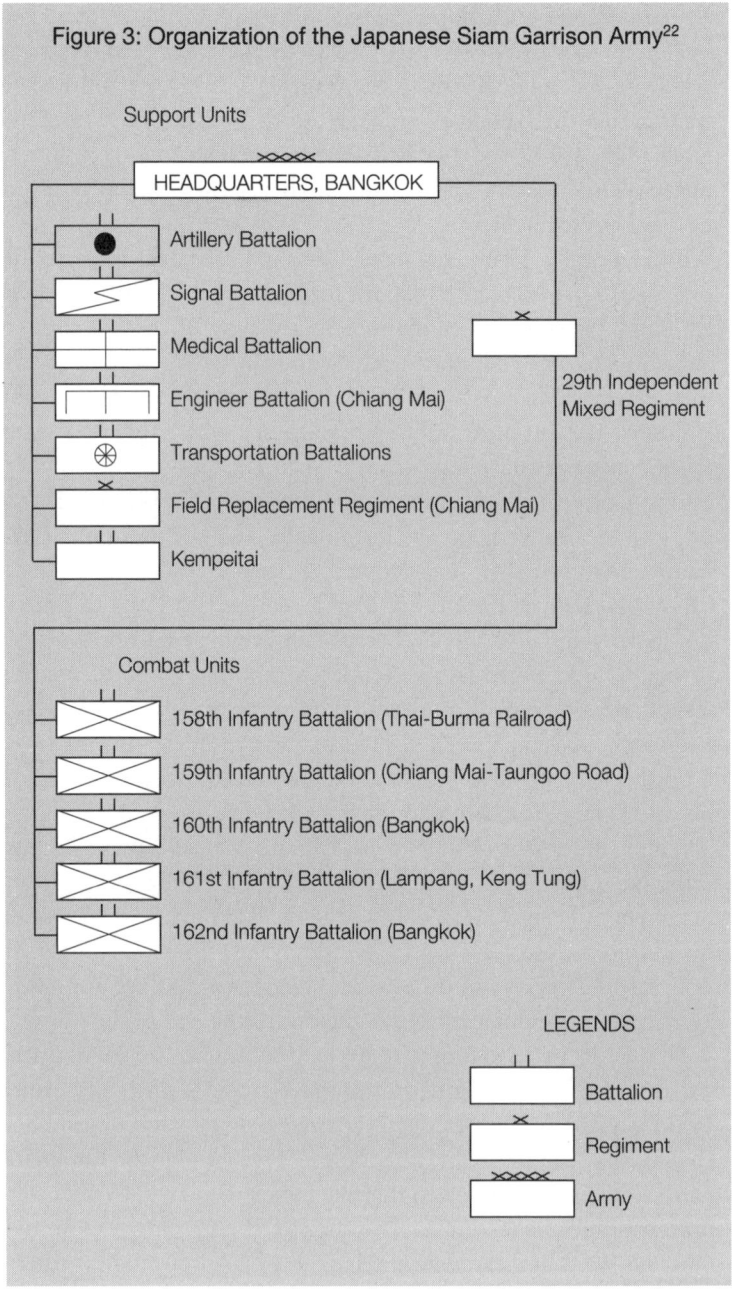

Figure 3: Organization of the Japanese Siam Garrison Army[22]

picture of resistance activities. Luang Suphachalasai believed that the Japanese knew about 60 percent of the resistance movement's activities, including that the underground was receiving agents, equipment, and communications from the Allies. They also knew that agents were entering Thailand by air, sea, and land, but not where or when.[23]

Smith and Clark mention in passing that the Japanese had captured five Thai attempting to infiltrate and Puay writes that some Chinese were captured by the Japanese. There is no available confirmation of these accounts and the Japanese reports of the period do not report that their forces captured any infiltrating agents.

Although overall Japanese security efforts were weak, they were, after all, dealing with an "ally." Large-scale counterintelligence and security efforts against the Thai populace held low priority. Nevertheless, the threat of such retaliatory activity was real, and it forced the underground to move cautiously and slowly in expanding its provincial operations.

THE WIDER POLITICAL ENVIRONMENT

During the period in which the resistance movement was consolidating its strength and political power in Thailand, events occurred outside the country that had a direct political effect on the Thai. The policies that the United States and Britain held toward the Thai government, in conflict since the start of the war, began to hinder Allied planning for the postwar period. The United States, attempting to forge a bond of Allied cooperation for wartime settlement, ran into stubborn British opposition to a guaranteed free Thailand.

In a series of diplomatic exchanges with the British Foreign Office, the U.S. State Department emphasized its sympathy for Thailand and urged the British to modify their uncompromising stand. The British reluctantly acknowledged that the Thai resistance movement had some effect on their official policy toward Thailand, but remained obdurate. On 26 February 1944 the British ambassador to the United States delivered the text of a proposed declaration by the British government concerning Thailand that stated in part:

A country with a long traditional friendship with us has, though admittedly under pressure from Japan, betrayed that friendship . . . For these acts Thailand is already paying the price and will undoubtedly pay a yet heavier price as the war reaches her territories. It is still possible for the people of Thailand to do something to save themselves from the worst consequences of their betrayal, and they will be judged by the efforts that they make to redeem themselves from the position in which the action of their present regime has placed them. Like other countries in like case "They must work their passage home."[24]

The State Department, in urging England to modify this stand, replied to the proposed declaration with a statement of unconditional support for the Thai resistance movement and the Thai people. Concerning the British proposal, the United States stated that it would do more harm than good, and asked England to withdraw it. The State Department then issued its strongest statement of support regarding the future of Thailand:

We shall treat Thailand . . . as enemy occupied territory . . . The United States continues to regard Thailand as an independent state. We do not recognize the present Thai government [Phibun's]. We continue to recognize as "Minister of Thailand" the Thai Minister in Washington, who has denounced his government's cooperation with Japan. We regard with sympathy a free Thai movement in which the Thai Minister in Washington is a prominent figure. . .We favor restoration to Thailand of complete freedom as a sovereign state and we favor creation in Thailand of a government which will represent the free will of the Thai people.[25]

This was a ringing declaration of faith and support to the Thai underground. It made clear the importance of continued cultivation of the Allies to secure political freedom after the war. More important, it specifically delineated the "free Thai movement" as the most effective instrument for securing this goal. The meaning of the United States statement was not lost on the underground. Its delivery, early in 1944, served to spur the resistance leadership to further expansion of activity and may have been a major factor in Pridi's decision to force Phibun's resignation.

On 16 August 1944, U.S. Secretary of State Cordell Hull delivered instructions to Ambassador Winan in London that continued the pressure on the British to modify their stance on Thailand. Emphasizing the need for unanimity among the Allies, Hull urged Winan to make it clear to the British government that the British needed to make a policy statement to the effect that Thailand must be continued as an independent state. In unusually strong diplomatic language between friends, Secretary Hull told his ambassador to state: "that absence of a statement of British intentions with respect to Thailand causes considerable inconvenience to this Government . . . "26

The timing of this statement of support for Thailand, at virtually the same time the symbol of anti-Allied strength in Thailand (Phibun) was being forced to resign, is a diplomatic coincidence of ironic interest.

The strong American note prompted a reply from the British foreign secretary on 4 September 1944 which attempted to mollify the Americans but still showed a firm anti-Thai bias. Pertinent parts of that message include:

> We, like the United States, want to see the restoration of Siam after the war as a free, sovereign and independent State, subject only to its acceptance of such special arrangements for security or economic collaboration as may be judged necessary . . . we wish, as do the United States, to encourage the Siamese themselves to create the maximum difficulties for the Japanese and thus to make the maximum contribution to their own liberation . . . [but] while appreciating the possible advantages of Siam's resistance to the Japanese, His Majesty's Government do not rate its practical value very high . . . We feel, in fact, that if resistance is to be encouraged it may need a spur rather than a sugarplum.27

The letter continued to comment at length on the issue of Thai occupation of British colonial territory in Malaya and Burma.

In his reply to this note, Secretary Hull immediately seized on two points. First, that both the United States and England shared the desire that Thailand should be independent after the war. Second, he requested clarification of the "special arrangements" mentioned in the British note. At the same time, Hull supported the British position that Thailand had to return the territories taken from Malaya, Burma, and Cambodia.[28] The diplomatic exchanges continued until the end of the war, and extended into postwar diplomatic meetings with Thailand that are beyond the scope of this study. The point to be stressed here is that the United States viewed the Thai resistance movement in a highly favorable light, while England had a different opinion. These differences were known to Pridi and M.R. Seni and must have influenced their views toward the Allies in the final year of the war and afterwards.

AMERICAN INTELLIGENCE OFFICERS REACH BANGKOK

Both the United States and England were anxious to meet with representatives of the Thai underground. As early as December 1944, Lord Louis Mountbatten, commander in chief of the Allies' Southeast Asia Command in Ceylon, sent a message to Bangkok asking Pridi to send a military representative to Ceylon for high-level discussions. Pridi sent Direk Chaiyanam, Lieutenant General Luang Chat Nakrop (the Royal Thai Army chief of staff), and Puay Ungphakon to Kandy. He also asked Thanat Khoman to travel from the United States to attend the meeting.[29] Plans for the meeting failed because London persisted in its policy that the agenda include only military topics. Pridi canceled the meeting when the British refused to permit discussion of political matters involved in a possible postwar settlement.[30]

At almost the same time, Pridi and the OSS exchanged messages proposing a similar meeting with American representatives in Bangkok. The United States did not impose restrictions on agenda items and Pridi readily approved the request. In late January 1945 (either 25 or 28 January) Majors Richard Greenlee and John Wester arrived in Bangkok. Wester had been a businessman in prewar

Thailand, while Greenlee had been a member of OSS chief General William Donovan's law firm and was sent to provide an unbiased viewpoint.[31] The two men were flown to a landing point near Hua Hin and then rode a Thai Customs Service ship to Bangkok.[32] The meetings with Pridi were critical to the Thai resistance movement. From the discussions came agreement that training personnel and communications specialists would be sent to train guerrilla units in as many strategic locations as possible. The United States would provide the necessary arms and equipment needed to form an effective guerrilla force for the resistance movement.

Major Greenlee remained in Bangkok for five days. He was impressed with the wealth of intelligence gathered by the underground, and with Pridi's plans for training and equipping a guerrilla force. He decided that it was imperative that this information and the plans reach Washington, D.C. at once. He took many maps and charts, including the entire known Japanese military organization and disposition scheme, and Pridi's plans for organizing a guerrilla force. He also carried Pridi's gifts to President Roosevelt and OSS chief William Donovan—gold cigarette lighters engraved with the regent's royal motif.[33] General Donovan and President Roosevelt approved almost immediately the basic points of Pridi's plans. Meanwhile, John Wester remained in Bangkok to begin training the Thai underground in better methods of intelligence gathering and reporting and to act as the primary funnel of intelligence from Thailand to the Allies.

Pridi later made similar arrangements with the British through radio messages instead of personal meetings. In February 1945 he sent a delegation to Ceylon but its impact on Force 136 was lessened after the OSS "coup" in getting the first Western intelligence officers into Thailand. Movement of the Thai delegation to and from Ceylon, dubbed Operation Sequence, was the first attempt to send an official party from Thailand by air. Direk Chaiyanam led the delegation, which also included General Chat and Puay. Two White Elephant agents went to Ceylon with the party to assist in organizing a training program for the anticipated influx of Thai guerrilla unit leaders. The Thai delegation became "Violets," [34] while Direk received the code name "Omar," a designation he used for the rest of the war.[35]

Direk took with him copies of the same documents taken to Washington, D.C. by Major Greenlee. He also pressed forcibly for British recognition of a free and independent Thailand after the war, a policy declaration England still refused to make. The Thai delegation spent nine days in Ceylon and achieved several goals despite making no headway in changing the British policy toward Thailand's political future. The British representatives agreed to recognize the legitimacy of the Seri Thai as a resistance movement but refused to make any commitments for postwar policy decisions. England also agreed to an accelerated program to provide supplies, arms, and equipment to the underground, to be coordinated with the United States.[36]

The representatives of the British agencies at the meeting were unable to agree among themselves to send intelligence officers to Bangkok, much to the chagrin of Force 136. They must have been embarrassed to learn that the OSS already had a man in the capital. At least the British agencies had begun to moderate their obdurate stand against Thailand from a political standpoint.

The Thai representatives in Ceylon did not attain all they wanted, but were satisfied with the results of the meeting. On the military side, Lord Mountbatten's representatives approved most of Pridi's guerrilla force planning and prepared for tripartite coordination among Thailand, England, and the United States to carry out its proposals. Lord Mountbatten's position as commander of the Southeast Asia Command made it logical for his staff to assume that responsibility.

ARMS, EQUIPMENT, PERSONNEL, AND TRAINING AUGMENT THE RESISTANCE MOVEMENT

The OSS and Force 136 had determined to enlarge the scope of their operations in Thailand before Greenlee's dramatic mission to Bangkok and Washington, D.C. Both agencies were encouraged by the underground organization in Thailand. By 1945 the two agencies were willing to put aside parochial concerns and cooperate in future endeavors in Thailand.

Before September 1944, parachuting of agents and equipment into Thailand was limited to sites near Hua Hin in the south, and in the mountainous regions ringing the central plains. The establishment of agents and reliable communications in Thailand made it logical to increase the amount of equipment sent into the country and to establish other secure landing sites.

Force 136 sent the first expanded load of arms and equipment to Thailand in early November 1944. Krit Totsayanon led a team of seven Thai guerrilla recruits to the new site at Sam Roi Yot, south of Hua Hin. A British plane dropped eleven parachutes with supplies, arms, equipment, and ammunition, as well as revised maps of Thailand and Burma. The inclusion of a large number of Sten and Bren guns for the new guerrilla movement was the first such shipment of arms to the resistance movement. The reception team recovered all of the equipment and took it to Bangkok for future dispersal to field units.[37] The operation was so successful that it became a model for future activities. Dozens of similar drops were conducted from that time on.

The resistance movement established a standard reception procedure. Each drop of agents or equipment was made at a site prearranged by radio contacts, with an on-site reception party of local underground or guerrilla leaders. Arrangement of these rendezvous sites and times involved a complicated but effective security check of communications procedures to insure that the agents in Thailand were not operating under enemy duress. From time to time one or more of the Allied agents acted as chief of a reception party, but usually the resistance used its own personnel. Reception teams posed as government inspection teams or policemen. In most cases the team members had plausible reasons to be in the areas concerned. No Thai reception team was ever compromised.[38]

As part of the program to expand resistance operations, the underground requested that the Allies use drop zones in other areas of Thailand where guerrilla or underground units were established and able to provide necessary security. Force 136 planned to establish a major delivery site for guerrilla forces on the Phu Kradung plateau in Loei province. However, the first agents sent to Thailand for this purpose had to be transferred to central Thailand because the underground had not established a reception base at Phu Kradung.

Operation Coupling, Force 136's code name for operations into northeast Thailand, began with the dispatch of three White Elephants—Praphot Paorohit (Nun), Thep Semthiti (Nu), and Sano Ninkhamhaeng (Chieu). Puay Ungphakon was sent from Bangkok as chief of their reception team. They established communications with Force 136, and then moved in a police vehicle convoy to the Phu Kradung area. This remote base rapidly became the major British operational airfield in Thailand.[39]

Operation Coupling continued its activities into January 1945. Pridi assigned Tiang Sirikhan (Pluto) to take charge of underground operations in that area. Tiang received a government contract to build a highway across the Phu Phan mountains between Sakon Nakhon and Kalasin provinces. He used the construction project to cover his location of a number of good rendezvous sites and training camps for guerrilla forces. Krit Totsayanon accompanied Tiang as a radio operator and liaison contact with British intelligence. They used Thai Highway Department equipment to move their equipment and to construct training camps throughout the remote hills of northeast Thailand.[40] This use of government equipment and missions to cover resistance activities became routine after Khuang became prime minister. Once Tiang and Krit were securely established the British made many drops of arms and equipment for the guerrillas in the provinces of Sakon Nakhon, Kalasin, and Nakhon Phanom.

While Force 136 was expanding into northeast Thailand at Phu Kradung and Sakon Nakhon, the OSS selected Phu Khiao as its major training and infiltration base. With rapid expansion the resistance soon had the legal air force field well secured, and it became a routine landing site for cargo and passenger flights into Thailand. Phu Khiao became the central staging area for transshipment of equipment to Bangkok or other field locations.[41] In the spring of 1945 OSS sent Major Alexander Griswold to Phu Khiao as chief of operations. Cargo and passengers for Bangkok were dropped at Phu Khiao by American pilots, then picked up by Thai aircraft and taken to Don Mueang Air Base for further distribution. Supplies for camps in northern and northeastern Thailand were delivered by Thai military convoy.[42]

British and American intelligence agencies cooperated in southern Thailand by establishing an island base in the Andaman Sea. Both agencies responded to Admiral Mountbatten's need for better intelligence on Japanese activities in southern Burma and western Thailand. USN Lieutenant William Horrigan was the project officer for finding a suitable base site. Initially he wanted to place an intelligence listening post on Davis Island, off the coast of the major Japanese naval base at Victoria Point, the southernmost point in Burma. Davis Island was too exposed to Japanese observation so he selected Chan Island, further south off the coast of Ranong province. A party of four Americans and two Thai agents, led by USN Lieutenant John Calhoun, landed at this base in December.[43]

Calhoun's missions were to watch and report on Japanese shipping along the west coast of Thailand and Burma and to establish liaison with the Thai resistance movement on the nearby mainland. In January 1945 another seven men were sent to Chan Island, by that time nicknamed "Chance Island," which became a major transshipment point for southern Thailand. Most equipment sent into Thailand's southern third passed through Chan Island. Thai agents and guerrillas traveling between Thailand and India also used the island as a relay point. The Thai resistance movement used customs service ships to ferry men and equipment to and from the mainland, while Catalina flying boats used the island's sheltered waters. Chan Island played an important role in the training of Thai guerrillas and as a transhipment point. However, it was finally compromised to the Japanese when enemy patrol planes spotted two parachutes entangled in trees. The island was safely evacuated in the spring of 1945.[44]

OFFSHORE TRAINING OF THAI RESISTANCE PERSONNEL

Force 136 initiated the first operation to take selected Thai resistance personnel to Ceylon and India for training in guerrilla operations and intelligence collection. This mission was dubbed Operation Influx, and the trainees were called "Browns" and "Blacks."[45] The first group of eight trainees met a Catalina in January 1945 at a rendezvous point near Tarutao Island off the southwest coast of Thailand. All eight of the trainees were police officers stationed in southern Thailand. The British selected them first to obtain current information on that region, a blank spot in the flow of intelligence from Thailand. Force 136 officers debriefed the men and sent them to a training camp near Colombo for intensive guerrilla training. After returning to Thailand with the code names of birds they became major underground leaders. For instance, the new chief of police in Phuket province was "Petrel."[46]

OSS also started training programs for the Thais by expanding existing programs in India. Nicol Smith was ordered to close his operation in Szemao. He and the remaining agents in China moved to Ceylon to train Thai agent trainees sent by the resistance. OSS reasoned that overland infiltration from China was no longer necessary, because men and equipment could be landed more easily by planes in Thailand.

Both the OSS and Force 136 had a language problem in their training programs, for most of the new trainees did not speak English. The Thai agents brought from India and China were therefore well suited for training the new Thai agent trainees. They not only had knowledge of intelligence and guerrilla operations, but could teach in the Thai language.

OSS and Force 136 quickly established small training camps in Ceylon and India to which the Thai underground sent a continual flow of men for guerrilla training. Both the United States and England sent special flights of Catalinas to pick up and return the trainees. Most OSS training took place at Smith's new camp near Trincomalee, Ceylon.[47] Most Force 136 personnel trained near Colombo. The two agencies cooperated to insure that the training given the Thai was similar. They also coordinated their supporting flights and later operations so the Japanese were not saturated with possible targets as the Thai returned to their country. Most of the offshore trainees were able to provide their families and neighbors with a cover story during their absence. Most recruits, either students or policemen, told their friends and family that they were busy with their studies or had been sent on special operations. Reports vary on the number of Thais sent for training in Ceylon and India during the first nine months of 1945. Popular histories of the period credit the intelligence agencies with training "hundreds" of Thais at offshore sites. Colonel Net Khemayothin, who spent two months (March to May 1945) as liaison officer with Force 136, has provided some useful figures. He visited with more than eighty Thai trainees from the military services, police, and universities in schools in India and Ceylon. He estimated that an equal number of Thai were trained in American-run camps.[48] His observations of the training camps would support an estimate of between two and three hundred Thai personnel trained in offshore sites between January and August 1945.

SUMMARY OF RESISTANCE EXPANSION AND RECEPTION OF ALLIED OFFICERS

By 1945 the Thai resistance movement had expanded from a small inner circle of Thai friends of Pridi Banomyong to a large organization with members in most parts of the country. Many members of the armed forces, the police, and the civil service supplemented Pridi's civilian friends. These elements of the underground leadership had initiated large-scale recruitment of a guerrilla force centered around regional centers established by provincial underground leaders.

Large field units had been established at Hua Hin under Chan Bunnak, at Phu Kradung under Udom Bunyaprakop and with British participation, and at Sakon Nakhon under Tiang Sirikhan. The Americans established their major base at Phu Khiao under Alexander Griswold, with a secondary base on Chan Island under John Calhoun. The resistance movement controlled almost all key positions in the central government and sympathetic men were assigned by the appropriate ministries to positions in the provinces. The underground controlled the expansion of its membership through routine administrative assignments. Gradually, however, these precautions began to arouse Japanese suspicions. The Thai resistance movement was no longer a small political unit. It had guerrilla units throughout the country under recruitment, supplemented by strong leaders and well-supplied with Allied arms and equipment. Allied intelligence officers had entered Bangkok and arrangements had been completed for Allied personnel to infiltrate Thailand to train the guerrilla units. OSS intelligence officers had established quarters in Bangkok to supervise intelligence collection operations and to conduct daily liaison contacts with the underground leadership.

A significant expansion of contacts with the Allies was also underway. Large numbers of selected Thai civilians and police were sent outside the country for training. When they returned to Thailand, they entered key positions in the national infrastructure. Allied agents were collecting and passing information to their headquarters for use in planning operations, targeting for bombing raids, and assessing the military and political climate inside Thailand and Japan.

Pridi Banomyong had furnished the United States and England with copies of a major proposal for anti-Japanese military operations in Thailand. Allied headquarters was actively engaged in finalizing those plans. In short, the Thai resistance movement was now ready for final offensive operations with the Allies against the Japanese in Thailand.

CHAPTER SIX

CONSOLIDATION, WAR PLANS, AND VICTORY, 1945

RESISTANCE ACTIVITIES IN BANGKOK

At the beginning of 1945 the resistance leadership in Thailand had two primary goals: first, to continue preparations for conventional military and guerrilla warfare against Japanese forces in Thailand; second, to plan for eventual conflict with Japan through coordinated action with Allied headquarters in Ceylon. The underground was fully aware of the political importance of the resistance effort to a favorable postwar settlement. Political objectives began to play an increasingly important role in the larger realm of international relations between Thailand and the Allies. The resistance movement placed emphasis on the methods by which those goals were to be achieved.

The task of preparing for warfare against Japanese forces took a variety of forms. Guerrilla leaders had to fill out their units with recruits. American and British agents continued to arrive in Thailand for assignments in Bangkok as well as in the provinces. Western intelligence officers arrived for liaison and training duties. Guerrilla training inside Thailand, as well as at offshore training sites, needed to be increased. Both Western and Thai instructors expanded training in subjects like low-intensity operations such as subversion, sabotage, and espionage against the Japanese. The underground received heavy tonnages of arms and equipment in a variety of modes and distributed the materials throughout the country. The internal command structure of the resistance movement required revamping to cope with this shift to large-scale activity and increased strengths and assets. Coordinated planning between Thailand and the Allies took place in both Bangkok and Ceylon. Pridi concerned himself with strategic plans and with the cumbersome process of coordination with the Allies. He was also concerned about the growing difficulties of commanding the resistance movement which, by 1945, had grown from a few trusted friends to thousands of Thais and Allies in numerous locations. Finally, the resistance had to function effectively under growing Japanese suspicion and apprehension.

The Allied agent population in Bangkok had grown to the point that it was no longer possible or practical for all Thai agents to live in one place. It was logical for them to assume a greater role in preparing the resistance movement for the coming struggle against the Japanese. Several of the agents were assigned to guerrilla camps in the provinces or to begin to set up new intelligence nets in other parts of the country.

John Wester set up the first new base of Allied operations outside the Santiban headquarters building. Originally he lived in an old palace on Phra Athit Road, near Pridi's official residence. The Thais reasoned correctly that the Japanese would not suspect that Americans were living and working in downtown Bangkok. OSS moved its Thailand headquarters to Suan Kulap Palace, Marshal Phibun's former official residence.

All American officers and agents in Bangkok were told to respect the position of the Regent and the authority of Thai government officials. They were to carry out their duties in strict cooperation with Pridi. The official declassified OSS history outlines the American mission in Bangkok in this way:

> OSS should look upon the Regent as the head of a friendly state and the chief of all clandestine activities in his area. The Siamese were to be supplied, advised, prodded, but no attempt should be made to create a separate American organization in the country. Everything must be done through the Siamese underground movement.[1]

The United States wanted its Allies to realize that the Thai government had official American support. This policy also encouraged the Thai resistance movement to continue its efforts against the Japanese with the implied approval of the United States. Pridi diversified his communications efforts by providing safe base stations for the Allies. Force 136 maintained its main radio station at the Santiban building, apparently under the control of Puay Ungphakon.[2] The British agents later established another station in a private home in Thonburi, under the supervision of Prasoet Pathummanon. OSS communications in the Santiban building were handled by Wimon Wiriyawit, Phisut Suthat, and Phunphoem Krairoek, all of whom worked through the police liaison system. When the OSS moved its operational headquarters to the Suan Kulap Palace the radio station followed.

OSS policy in Thailand placed intelligence collection in first priority, ahead of guerrilla training and clandestine operations. The lack of details in the information reported from Bangkok was a prime reason for sending American officers into Thailand. In contrast, British intelligence officers were more interested in establishing and training guerrilla units for clandestine operations against Japanese military forces. The first British officers in Thailand were sent directly to training sites in the provinces in the early spring of 1945. The British did not station a full-time officer in Bangkok until May of that year.

The British had posted Major Arun to Bangkok for a short liaison visit early in 1945. In May they launched Operation Pannicle whose purpose was to send a full liaison team to work directly with Pridi. Brigadier Victor M. Jacques, a long-time prewar resident of Bangkok, led the team. His duties were to act as a political representative of Admiral Mountbatten and to conduct liaison with underground leaders. He located his headquarters near Pridi's home and established regular contacts with John Wester and his successors.

By March 1945 Pridi had a firm staff organization to assist him in directing the resistance movement. The staff assumed responsibility for four aspects of resistance operations. First, they finalized the structure of the underground organization in Bangkok and the provinces. Pridi retained political power and ultimate political decision-making responsibility. Second, the staff conducted daily operational planning and underground activities. Third, the staff assisted the Allied agents in communicating with Ceylon and India and in planning and coordinating forthcoming operations against the Japanese. Finally, Pridi and his staff continued to plan for post-war political complications and to advise Prime Minister Khuang.

UNDERGROUND CONSOLIDATION

With a staff conducting the daily operations of the resistance movement (see figure 4), Pridi was freed to concentrate on political issues. The staff, in turn, consolidated its command of the resistance movement's provincial elements through control of the government infrastructure. Seri Thai members held posts as ministers of education, public health, and interior. These three agencies had centralized assignment responsibility for such key positions as

Figure 4. The Thai Underground Functional Staff [4]

NAME	CODE NAME	POSITION
Pridi Banomyong	Ruth	Chief of the resistance
Police General Adun Adundetcharat		
	Betty	Deputy chief of the resistance; commander, national police
Direk Chaiyanam	Omar	Chief of personnel; chief of interior
Wichit Lulitanon	unknown	Chief quartermaster; deputy chief of interior
Thawi Bunyaket	unknown	Chief of political affairs; liaison to government
Chan Bunnak	C-One	Chief of security; chief of communications; chief of reception and dispatch
Luang Banakon Kowit	unknown	Chief of boat operations
Saphrang Thep-hatsadin	unknown	Chief of land operations
General Luang Chit Mansin Sinatyotharak		
	Champa	Chief of army forces
Rear Admiral Luang Sangwon Yuthakit		
	unknown	Chief of naval forces; chief of prisoner protection
Thawi Tawetikun	unknown	Chief of economics and finance

province governors, district officers, and most school teachers. By controlling these important infrastructure positions throughout the provinces the underground used the government structure to conduct resistance managerial tasks. Provincial officials were kept informed of resistance activities and were assigned to operational missions through their ministerial communications systems. Local officials and school teachers constantly sought suitable recruits for the guerrilla forces, especially those who could be sent for offshore training without causing undue concern at home.[3]

The membership totals for all guerrilla units in the provinces are not available, but some estimated strengths are listed in figure 5. The membership of the resistance movement, particularly the guerrilla forces, grew rapidly. One source estimated that in Bangkok alone there were over ten thousand guerrilla members available to supplement the regular army First Division. The guerrilla force was organized into five or more subunits on a geographical basis.[5]

The total strength of guerrilla forces formed and trained by August 1945 varies according to the source. One figure puts the total strength of the guerrillas between fifty and ninety thousand.[6] To this number must be added nearly all of the Thai regular armed

Figure 5. Estimated Size of Selected Guerrilla Units [8]

LOCATION	NUMBER OF MEMBERS
Chachoengsao	130
Chonburi	2,000
Hua Hin (Prachuap Khiri Khan)	1,000
Maha Sarakham	4,000
Nakhon Phanom	900
Nong Khai	200
Phetchaburi	4,300
Phu Khiao (Chaiyaphum)	250
Phu Kradung (Loei)	200
Sakon Nakhon	3,500
Ubon Ratchathani	3,000
Udon Thani	1,200
Uttaradit	5,000
Bangkok/Thonburi	10,000+

forces and the police. More members would have been available had the war lasted longer. For example, many Thai trainees were in Ceylon and India at the end of the war. Additional recruits were stationed at many guerrilla camps inside Thailand. The National Assembly, in July 1945, passed the Home Guard Law that would have mobilized all males between the ages of twenty and thirty. The government planned to divert them to the resistance movement.[7] If Thailand had gone to war against the Japanese, the country would have possessed a formidable force of military and paramilitary units.

EXPANSION OF RESISTANCE ACTIVITIES

Formation of a functional staff eased the problems of planning and conducting resistance operations against the Japanese. Arrival of Allied officers and the return of many Thai from offshore training brought new skills for the indoctrination of recruits. These men also facilitated international liaison and internal coordination insofar as guerrilla activities were concerned. The staff divided operational functions into two major areas of responsibility. One group handled all matters pertaining to training, including both domestic and overseas sites, selection and movement of trainees to and from offshore training sites, and assignment of areas of responsibility to the guerrilla units. A second staff group coordinated activities among the police, military services, and the civilian branches of the resistance movement. This group also conducted strategic military and political planning and collected intelligence for the Allies.[9]

The resistance movement staff also assigned responsibilities to specific Thai governmental agencies and their covert participation in the resistance movement. For example, the police had principal responsibility for intelligence collection and security matters. Provincial governors acted as chiefs of resistance activity in their provinces and were responsible for communications with guerrilla units under their control and with resistance headquarters in Bangkok. Deputy governors were responsible for logistical support of guerrilla units and training camps. Provincial directors of education supervised the school teachers to recruit new guerrilla members. They also had the mission to establish guerrilla cells in each village, with a minimum requirement of two cells per province, each with at least twenty-five members. District officers assisted in the recruitment process and selected trainees for training inside Thailand. Each province was required to have a special reception team to receive and distribute supplies to their guerrilla units.[10]

Communications and coordination between the various units of the resistance movement became very effective, especially after responsibilities were firmly delineated. Thawi Bunyaket, as the underground's liaison officer to the Thai government, met with members of the formal governmental infrastructure to coordinate resistance activities and to serve as a channel for information and new requirements. Evidence suggests that provincial resistance leaders obeyed the coordination instructions received. For example, Chiap Amphunan, the police captain who headed resistance activities in Chumphon province, was specifically told to avoid contact with friends in adjacent provinces. Although Chiap and his superiors in the resistance movement knew that they had friends on resistance missions in other areas, they were worried that careless comments might compromise sensitive underground operations.[11]

As guerrilla units became operative they received specific missions. Some were directed to provide security for airfields, bases, and training camps such as those at Phu Khiao, Phu Kradung, and Ban Phon (Sakon Nakhon). Other units stole Japanese gasoline, weapons, ammunition, equipment, and vehicles for use by the resistance movement.[12] The Allied commitment to arm and train guerrilla units brought hope that each major unit formed would receive Allied officers or non-commissioned officers to prepare the members for combat. Trained units would be commanded by Thai officers but would have Allied "advisers" and would respond to requirements sent from the Allied command on Ceylon. By maintaining a close degree of control over the resistance forces the Allies would have an effective guerrilla arm for use against the Japanese. At the same time the Thai would gain political favor with the Allies by providing their own people to assist Allied operations. This would perpetuate Pridi's political goals for the postwar settlements to come.

Map 4: Location of Resistance Teams with Only Thai Members

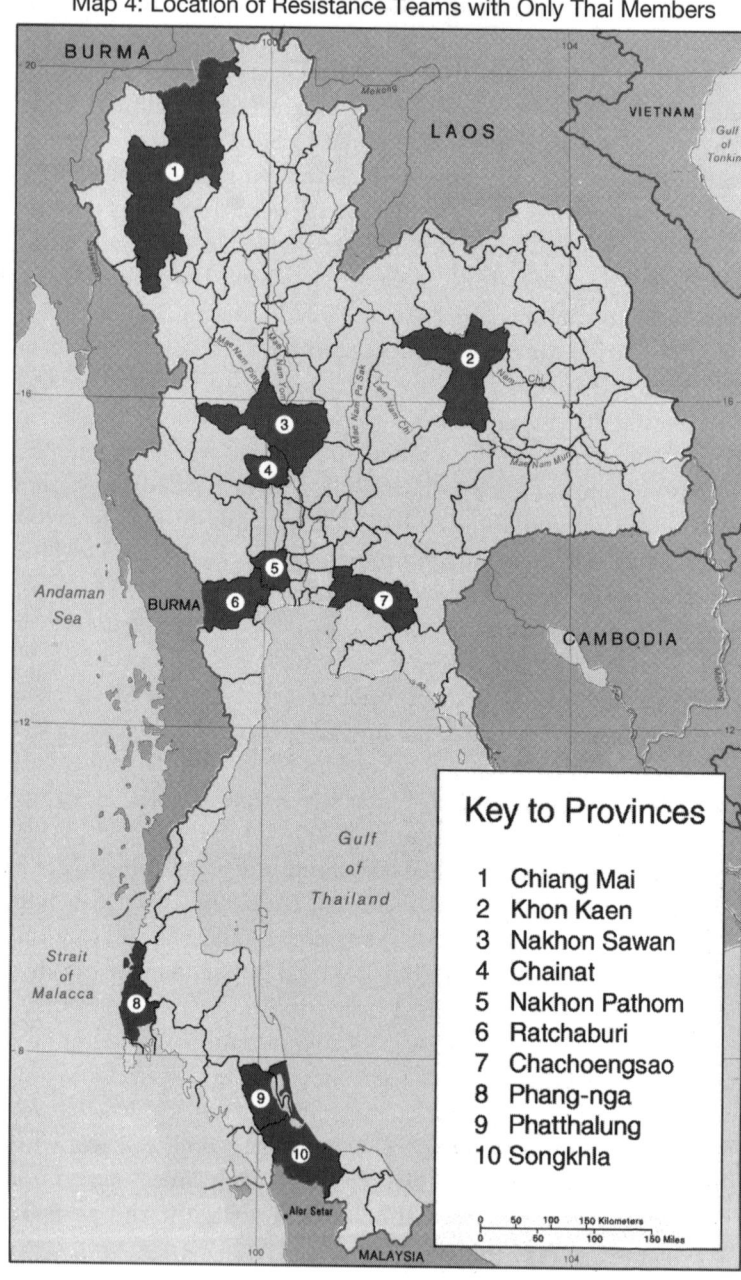

Key to Provinces

1 Chiang Mai
2 Khon Kaen
3 Nakhon Sawan
4 Chainat
5 Nakhon Pathom
6 Ratchaburi
7 Chachoengsao
8 Phang-nga
9 Phatthalung
10 Songkhla

Operationally the resistance leadership planned that American and British officers would not be stationed at camps in the same area. This policy would eliminate duplication of effort in sending men into Thailand and would also minimize the chance of overt political rivalry among the Allies. In those instances where overlapping of Allied personnel occurred (e.g. Sakon Nakhon), one force was responsible for training in a particular subject, while the other had different responsibilities such as security. Thai cadres and, in many instances, Allies as well, did not know the location of most other resistance units. However, all guerrilla units had direct radio contact with Bangkok. After arrival of Allied officers with more sophisticated equipment the camps also communicated directly with India and Ceylon. These procedures minimized duplication and maintained harmony among the various nationalities involved in the guerrilla effort. Placement of guerrilla management in the hands of capable leaders freed Bangkok personnel to concentrate on intelligence collection and reporting and liaison duties without the added burden of commanding the guerrilla training effort.

American and British intelligence officers arrived in Thailand throughout the spring of 1945. Efforts were made to distribute the Allied officers throughout the country, but not every province or resistance camp received them (see map 4). In May, Major Alexander Griswold took over control of operations at the Phu Khiao airstrip. M.C. Yuthitsathian Sawatdiwat, one of the original twenty-one agents first stationed at Szemao, acted as Griswold's assistant. They were met at Phu Khiao by Charoen Watthanaphanit who had arrived in Thailand some months earlier. The first OSS bases established solely for training Thai guerrilla forces were near Kanchanaburi. U.S. Navy Lieutenant Ettore H. A. "Bud" Grassi and Somchit Kangsanon parachuted into the province to establish the complex of several camps in that province. Three more Americans later arrived to help run the other camps.[13] Other Americans established training facilities near Phetchaburi, Chonburi, and Sakon Nakhon. One of the more unusual missions was given to the OSS training team at Khlong Phai where Captain Wayne Mumma trained a unit of Thai convicts.[14]

British officers began to arrive in Thailand during the spring of

Map 5: Infiltration Routes of Allied Intelligence Officers, Summer 1944

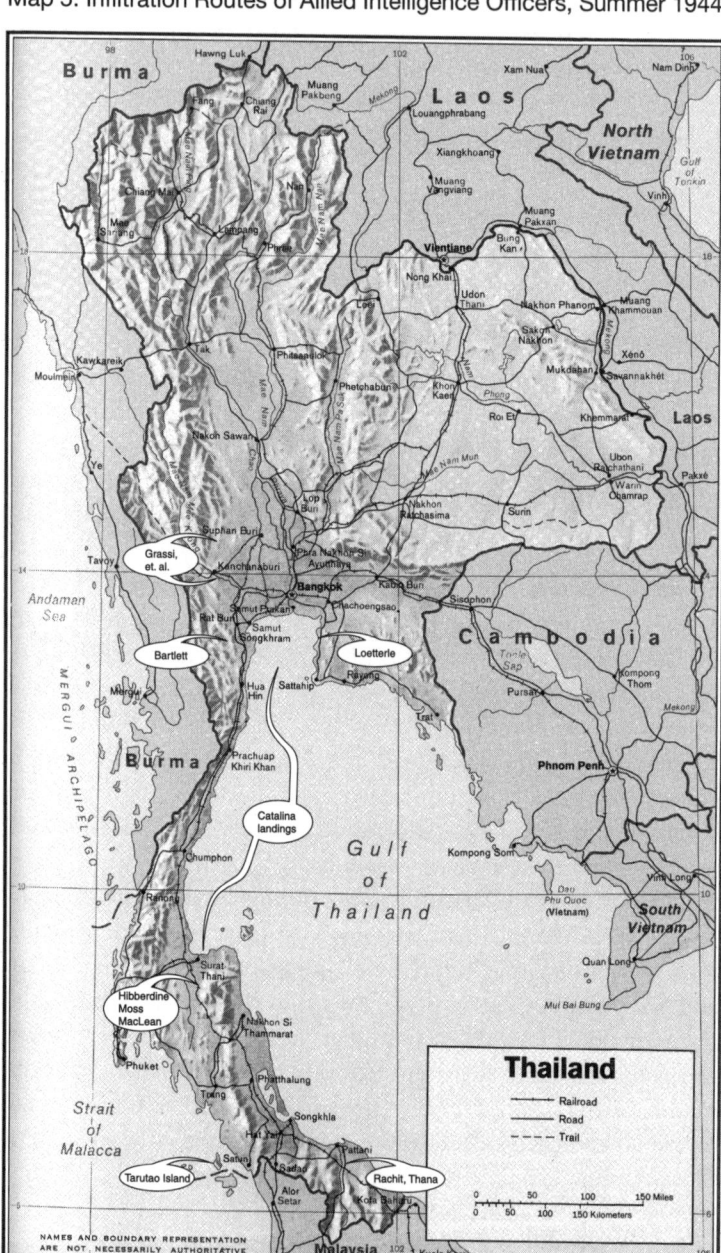

1945. Their first camp was at Ban Phon in Sakon Nakhon province, where Major David Smiley supervised the training of guerrillas. Several additional British officers, who reached Ban Phon a few days after the Japanese surrender, were charged to receive the local surrender of Japanese forces and to conduct liaison with friendly forces across the Mekong River in Laos.[15] In southern Thailand another small group of British officers landed in Surat Thani province to conduct training and to disrupt the north-south railroad. These officers (Captain John Hibberdine and W. Stanley Moss) were met by the commander of the Thai army's Sixth Division and by three White Elephants (Prem, Samran, and Major Arun) who had been reassigned from Bangkok. (The infiltration routes of most British and American personnel are shown in map 5.) This group had similar instructions regarding the Japanese surrender. Rosters of American and British intelligence officers known to have served in Thailand during World War II are as complete as available information permits (see figures 6 and 7).

Figure 6. Americans Who Served with the Thailand Resistance Movement

LOCATION	NAMES
Bangkok	Major John Wester, Major James Thompson, Major Richard Greenlee, Lt Col Nicol Smith, Captain Howard Palmer, Lt Cdr Alexander MacDonald, Lloyd George
Chonburi province	Captain Francis G. Loetterle
Phu Khiao base	Major Alexander B. Griswold
Kanchanaburi province	Harry Olwell, Edward Arida, James J. Hogan Jr., Lieutenant Ettore H. A. "Bud" Grassi
Petchaburi province	Major Eben Bartlett, Sergeant Gallager
Khlong Phai prison team	Captain Wayne Mumma, Petty Officer Warren Gilbertson
Sakhon Nakhon	Major John Holliday (also reported to have served in Chiang Mai)
Chan Island	Lieutenant John Calhoun, Captain David H. Blee, Lieutenant Cleveland Autrey, Private Glenn
Location unidentified	Gerald L. Bennatto, Lieutenant Howard T. Bush, Sergeant Howard R. Costa, William Davis, S. Dillon Ripley, Sergeant Kenneth E. Hughes, Lambert A. Smith, Sergeant S. J. Sysko, Commander Edward Taylor

Figure 7. British Who Served with the Thailand Resistance Movement

LOCATION	NAMES
Bangkok	Brigadier Victor H. Jacques, Major Thomas Hobbs
Surat Thani province	Captain W. Stanley Moss, Captain John Hibberdine, William MacLean
Tak province	Major Brightsmith
Yala province	Major E. A. Hasler
Sakon Nakhon province	Major David Smiley, Major Peter Kemp, Captain Towland Winn, Sergeant "Spider" Lawson, Sergeant Collins
Phu Kradung base	R. Hudson

By the summer of 1945, scores of American and British agents and Allied officers had entered Thailand by air, sea, overland, and by parachute (see maps 6 and 7). Once in Thailand they received extensive support from the local populace and the resistance infrastructure at the provincial and district levels. M.C. Karawik Chakraphan recognized the importance of local assistance when he wrote: "Guerrilla and subversive activities would have been well-nigh impossible had it not been for the organization inside Siam. In rural districts a stranger is recognized at a glance. Without local help we would not have lasted long."[16]

The resistance movement made efficient use of equipment sent by the Allies. Sten and Bren guns and American carbines went directly to guerrilla units, including units in areas where no Allied officers were stationed. Plastic explosives, blasting caps, and grenades were sent to the guerrillas as well as to underground members in Bangkok. Radios enabled each camp to maintain contact with Allied headquarters and with resistance headquarters in Bangkok. Both the United States and England insisted that the resistance movement issue the new weapons only to guerrilla units and underground leaders. It would have been politically unacceptable to allow Allied weapons to be used by the regular Thai armed forces. Pridi agreed with this decision.[17]

Recovery and distribution of supplies became a routine procedure. Some equipment airdrops, however, were exciting. On one mission three American airplanes in support of the resistance

Map 6: Location of American Teams in Support of the Resistance

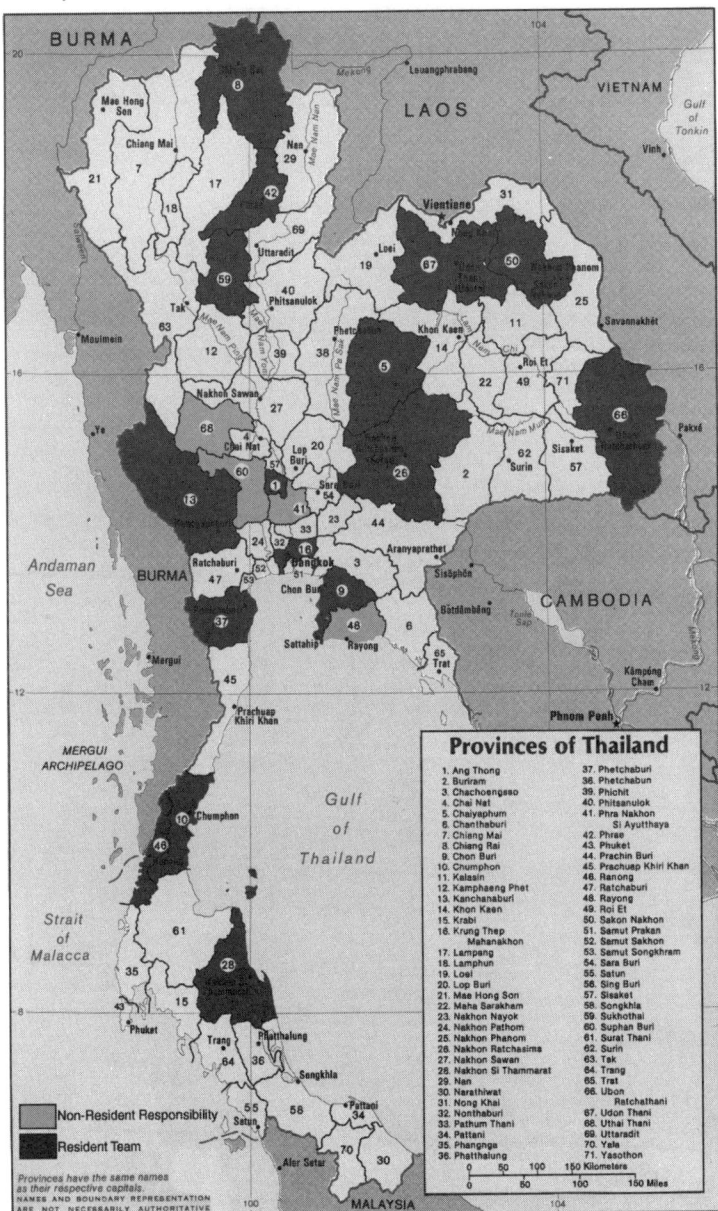

Provinces of Thailand

1. Ang Thong	37. Phetchaburi
2. Buriram	38. Phetchabun
3. Chachoengsao	39. Phichit
4. Chai Nat	40. Phitsanulok
5. Chaiyaphum	41. Phra Nakhon
6. Chanthaburi	Si Ayutthaya
7. Chiang Mai	42. Phrae
8. Chiang Rai	43. Phuket
9. Chon Buri	44. Prachin Buri
10. Chumphon	45. Prachuap Khiri Khan
11. Kalasin	46. Ranong
12. Kamphaeng Phet	47. Ratchaburi
13. Kanchanaburi	48. Rayong
14. Khon Kaen	49. Roi Et
15. Krabi	50. Sakon Nakhon
16. Krung Thep	51. Samut Prakan
Mahanakhon	52. Samut Sakhon
17. Lampang	53. Samut Songkhram
18. Lamphun	54. Sara Buri
19. Loei	55. Satun
20. Lop Buri	56. Sing Buri
21. Mae Hong Son	57. Sisaket
22. Maha Sarakham	58. Songkhla
23. Nakhon Nayok	59. Sukhothai
24. Nakhon Pathom	60. Suphan Buri
25. Nakhon Phanom	61. Surat Thani
26. Nakhon Ratchasima	62. Surin
27. Nakhon Sawan	63. Tak
28. Nakhon Si Thammarat	64. Trang
29. Nan	65. Trat
30. Narathiwat	66. Ubon
31. Nong Khai	Ratchathani
32. Nonthaburi	67. Udon Thani
33. Pathum Thani	68. Uthai Thani
34. Pattani	69. Uttaradit
35. Phangnga	70. Yala
36. Phatthalung	71. Yasothon

Non-Resident Responsibility

Resident Team

Provinces have the same names
as their respective capitals.
NAMES AND BOUNDARY REPRESENTATION
ARE NOT NECESSARILY AUTHORITATIVE

Map 7: Location of British Teams in Support of the Resistance

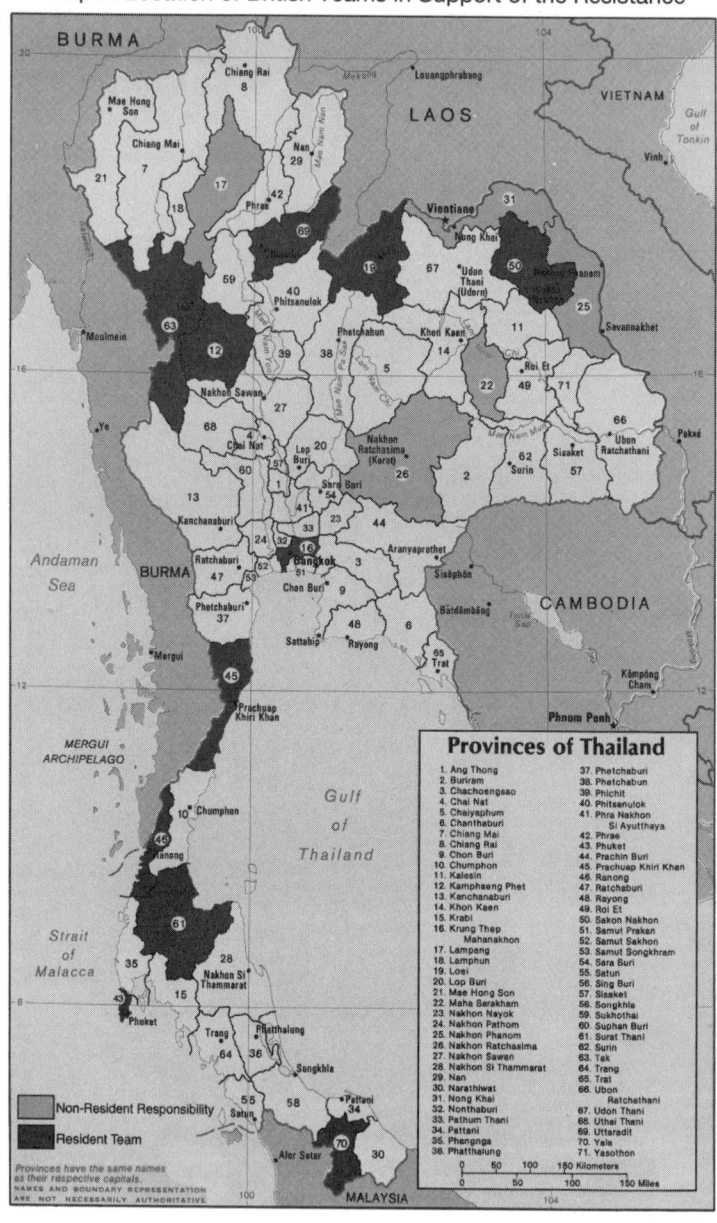

dropped dozens of packages of medicines and equipment at Sanam Luang (Pramane Grounds) in the heart of Bangkok. The drop was largely for propaganda purposes, to demonstrate to the Japanese as well as the Thai populace the pinpoint capabilities of Allied bombers. Santiban policemen were notified in advance of the drop, retrieved the supplies in broad daylight, and escaped before the surprised Japanese arrived. Another time an American airplane landed with a cargo of radio equipment at Khok-krathiam, near Lopburi. Resistance forces loaded the equipment in Thai army trucks and drove past an oncoming Japanese inspection team without incident.[18] By the end of the war an estimated 200 tons of arms and materiel had been delivered to Thailand by air.[19]

While most of the arms awaited the coming of anticipated joint operations, on occasion guerrillas attacked small and isolated Japanese patrols. In early March 1945, for example, a force of over a hundred guerrillas ambushed a Japanese river convoy between Lampang and Tak in northern Thailand. They killed fourteen Japanese soldiers and seized a quantity of small arms and ammunition.

The furious Japanese commander in Bangkok insisted on an investigation and punishment of the attackers. Thai officials stalled the investigation until the guerrillas had escaped.[20] OSS intelligence reported fourteen similar ambushes[21] and doubtless there were more.

Adequate documentation is lacking on one activity popularly credited to the Thai resistance movement. Some reports indicate that "hundreds" of Allied pilots were rescued by the Thais and moved to safety. However, few such incidents are reported in the sources examined. In early 1944 General Claire Chennault personally asked Nicol Smith (then at Szemao) if his sources in Bangkok could locate William McGarry, a pilot believed to have crashed in Thailand in 1942. Smith radioed the request to Bangkok. Four days later he received a reply that McGarry was in a prison camp under Japanese supervision but guarded by Thais. In time the underground contacted McGarry with an escape plan. McGarry feigned illness and then death. The underground moved him from the camp in a closed coffin. Later he was flown out of the country.[22]

This incident helped to establish the reputation of the underground as a genuine resistance movement, not a puppet organization controlled by the Japanese.[23]

In another incident a plane piloted by Major John Gildee was shot down by Japanese fighters in central Thailand. Resistance members reached the wreckage before the Japanese and spirited into hiding the surviving crew members. Later they were taken to Bangkok for emergency medical treatment and then flown out of Thailand.[24] A final example of this type of resistance activity involved a bomber that crashed near Nakhon Sawan in August 1944. Resistance cadres took the survivors to Phu Khiao for aerial evacuation to India.[25]

Martin has written that the resistance movement smuggled over four hundred Allied fliers and prisoners of war to remote resistance airstrips for evacuation from Thailand.[26] Nuechterlein reports that:

> The contribution of the Free Thai and the Thai underground to the Allied war effort was significant: it enabled British and American forces to penetrate Thailand, to obtain information on Japanese capabilities and troop movements, and to rescue *seven hundred* [italics added] American and British fliers who had been forced down over Thai territory.[27]

Several similar incidents are cited in the literature but data were not found to support these large numbers.

One last infiltration operation deserves mention. In early 1945 Allied headquarters planned to occupy Phuket Island as a prelude to the invasion and reoccupation of Malaya and Singapore. Force 136 launched Operation Priest to collect information on the region from the Kra Isthmus to the Malayan border. Bangkok released several British agents from duties in the capital to assist the operation, while two additional teams of agents were sent from Ceylon. Phetrachit Buri and Thana Potsayanon (both White Elephants) were flown by Thai air force planes and parachuted into Yala province.[28] Two Ceylon-based members of the original group of White Elephants (Watthana Chitwari and M.C. Phitsadet Ratchani) landed on Phuket Island. When Lord Mountbatten canceled the overall invasion plan the agents of Operation Priest turned their efforts to recruiting cadre for offshore training and collecting intelligence.[29] By then the active efforts of Allied and Thai resistance units covered almost all of the country (see map 8).

WAR PLANNING AND POLITICAL PREPARATION

The resistance plan for the participation of the Thai in a military offensive against the Japanese had five aspects. It involved the use of strategically located guerrilla units, conventional military forces concentrated at defensive points, control of Bangkok by the Thai army and local guerrillas, mobilization of police units throughout the country, and navy security operations along the seacoast. Pridi left the exact positioning of Thai forces to Lord Mountbatten's staff, since the Allied headquarters would control military operations in Thailand.

Cooperation among police, military, and civilian leaders became more crucial and, fortunately, was effective. On several occasions the underground sent liaison officers to Ceylon and India to insure that matters were coordinated between Thailand and the Allied command. General Sinatyotharak, responsible for the selection and dispatch of military liaison officers, sent Net Khemayothin to Ceylon and India for this purpose. He selected Colonel Net because of his prior service to Marshal Phibun in making contacts with the Chinese. Net spent two months observing the offshore training of Thai recruits. He returned to Thailand by air in June 1945.[30] At the same time that Net was acting as liaison officer to Force 136, the underground sent Colonel Thawi Chunlasap and Lieutenant Colonel Ekasak Praphanotyothin, respectively, as air force and army liaison officers to OSS.[31] Thawi's duties in Ceylon were to act as liaison officer to the Allied intelligence section. He read and interpreted aerial photographs of Thailand to assess bomb damage and to select targets for air force raids. He received additional training in intelligence and guerrilla operations, including a one-week trip to the United States. He accompanied American bombing missions over Thailand to pinpoint targets for air crews to insure

Map 8: Organizational Coverage of the Thai Resistance Movement

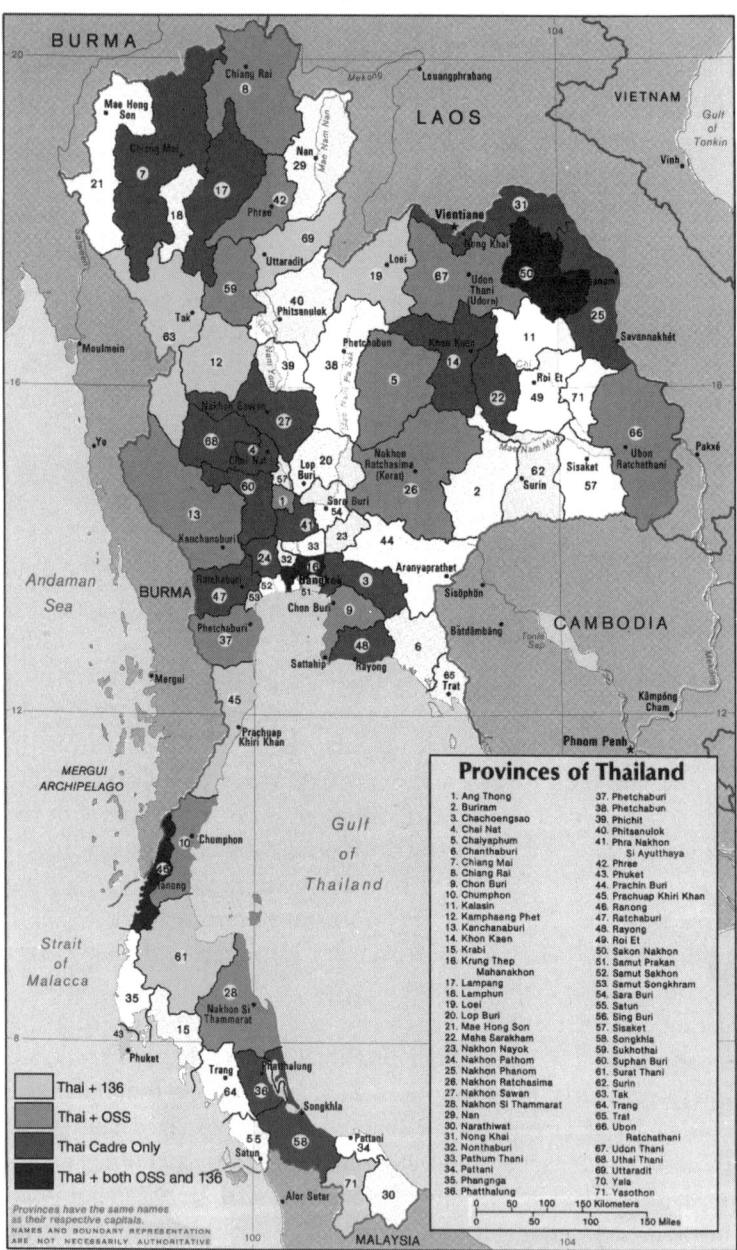

Provinces of Thailand

1. Ang Thong
2. Buriram
3. Chachoengsao
4. Chai Nat
5. Chaiyaphum
6. Chanthaburi
7. Chiang Mai
8. Chiang Rai
9. Chon Buri
10. Chumphon
11. Kalasin
12. Kamphaeng Phet
13. Kanchanaburi
14. Khon Kaen
15. Krabi
16. Krung Thep Mahanakhon
17. Lampang
18. Lamphun
19. Loei
20. Lop Buri
21. Mae Hong Son
22. Maha Sarakham
23. Nakhon Nayok
24. Nakhon Pathom
25. Nakhon Phanom
26. Nakhon Ratchasima
27. Nakhon Sawan
28. Nakhon Si Thammarat
29. Nan
30. Narathiwat
31. Nong Khai
32. Nonthaburi
33. Pathum Thani
34. Pattani
35. Phangnga
36. Phatthalung
37. Phetchaburi
38. Phetchabun
39. Phichit
40. Phitsanulok
41. Phra Nakhon Si Ayutthaya
42. Phrae
43. Phuket
44. Prachin Buri
45. Prachuap Khiri Khan
46. Ranong
47. Ratchaburi
48. Rayong
49. Roi Et
50. Sakon Nakhon
51. Samut Prakan
52. Samut Sakhon
53. Samut Songkhram
54. Sara Buri
55. Satun
56. Sing Buri
57. Sisaket
58. Songkhla
59. Sukhothai
60. Suphan Buri
61. Surat Thani
62. Surin
63. Tak
64. Trang
65. Trat
66. Ubon Ratchathani
67. Udon Thani
68. Uthai Thani
69. Uttaradit
70. Yala
71. Yasothon

Thai + 136
Thai + OSS
Thai Cadre Only
Thai + both OSS and 136

Provinces have the same names as their respective capitals.
NAMES AND BOUNDARY REPRESENTATION ARE NOT NECESSARILY AUTHORITATIVE

accuracy.[32] Harin Hongsakun, another Thai air force officer, went to India as liaison officer. Both Thawi and Harin later became air chief marshals in the Royal Thai Air Force and rose to positions of power in postwar governments.

As Japan's forces suffered increasing reverses during the spring of 1945, work on the Allied concept of operations for the Thai offensive progressed. All parties sensed the beginning of the end and morale was high. The plan, as finalized, called for Allied forces to enter Thailand from Burma at several locations. Thai forces were assigned missions to seize the major military bases in Bangkok, Kanchanaburi, and the Lopburi-Saraburi complex and to secure staging areas so Allied forces could flank Japanese forces withdrawing down the railroad from Three Pagodas Pass on the Burma border. Guerrilla units in the provinces were to cut Japanese lines of communication to Cambodia and Malaya and to harass troops throughout the country. Finally, the resistance was to attack local targets of opportunity and prevent Japanese forces from attacking or disarming Thai military units.[33]

The Thai army added several details to the plan. The First Division in Bangkok would seize the city in conjunction with underground forces, while the military strength in the Lopburi-Saraburi complex would be increased to one full division. Forces at Nakhon Sawan, Phitsanulok, and Sukhothai were to move south to prevent a Japanese withdrawal from northern Thailand. Small military elements in Tak, Phetchaburi, and Ratchaburi were to join with guerrilla units in those provinces to augment their strength. Units in Prachinburi and Chonburi would do the same in southeast Thailand. Regular and guerrilla forces in the northeast would cut highways and railroads and block any enemy advances from Laos and Cambodia.

While the Allied plan called for the bulk of Allied forces to enter Thailand from Burma, the United States planned supporting operations in southeast Thailand. The Americans planned to conduct naval operations off the Thai coast, with Marine landings at Trat, Sattahip, Chonburi, and Chantaburi.[34] The Thai government would retain control of guerrilla forces operating under the "supervision" of American or British training officers, but they would respond to the orders of their respective sponsoring national component within the Allied command. The main attack line expected from the Japanese was along the Taunggyi–Keng Tung–Chiang Mai–Lampang axis, with a secondary effort along the Thai-Burma railroad from Moulmein over Three Pagodas Pass toward Kanchanaburi (see map 9).

The resistance movement had completed its plans for a major contribution to the Allied war effort in Southeast Asia. The Allied command was relying on the assistance of the Thai military and guerrilla forces to make major inroads against Japanese combat units and supply bases and to tie down any attempts to reinforce the withdrawing Japanese army. At the same time, the Thai resistance forces, which expected to suffer heavy casualties, were prepared to make the sacrifice to improve their national image in the Allies' eyes.

JAPANESE SUSPICIONS, REACTIONS, AND DEFEAT

General Nakamura, the Japanese commander in Thailand, had general knowledge of many of the plans formulated by the resistance movement. He told various Thai government officials that he knew of their plans to confront Japan. He also was aware that the resistance had been infiltrating supporters and equipment at the borders as well as at secret airfields throughout the country.[35] Indeed, increased Japanese search efforts forced the resistance leadership to suspend Allied air landings and air drops in June 1945. Throughout this period the Japanese increased their efforts to determine the nature and scope of the exact plans of the resistance.

Events in early 1945 gave rise to real fears that the Japanese military command would seize the Thai government as they had done with the Vichy government in Indochina. Increased Japanese troop movements and construction of permanent supply depots added to the government's uneasiness. Japanese troops moved from Malaya to Kanchanaburi and Chumphon. Other units built airfields at Udon Thani and Ubon Ratchathani. Still other forces built storage facilities at Saraburi, Nakhon Nayok, and Prachinburi.[36] Pridi observed in a postwar interview: "We kept expecting the Japs

Map 9: Resistance Tactics Planned during Allied Offensive

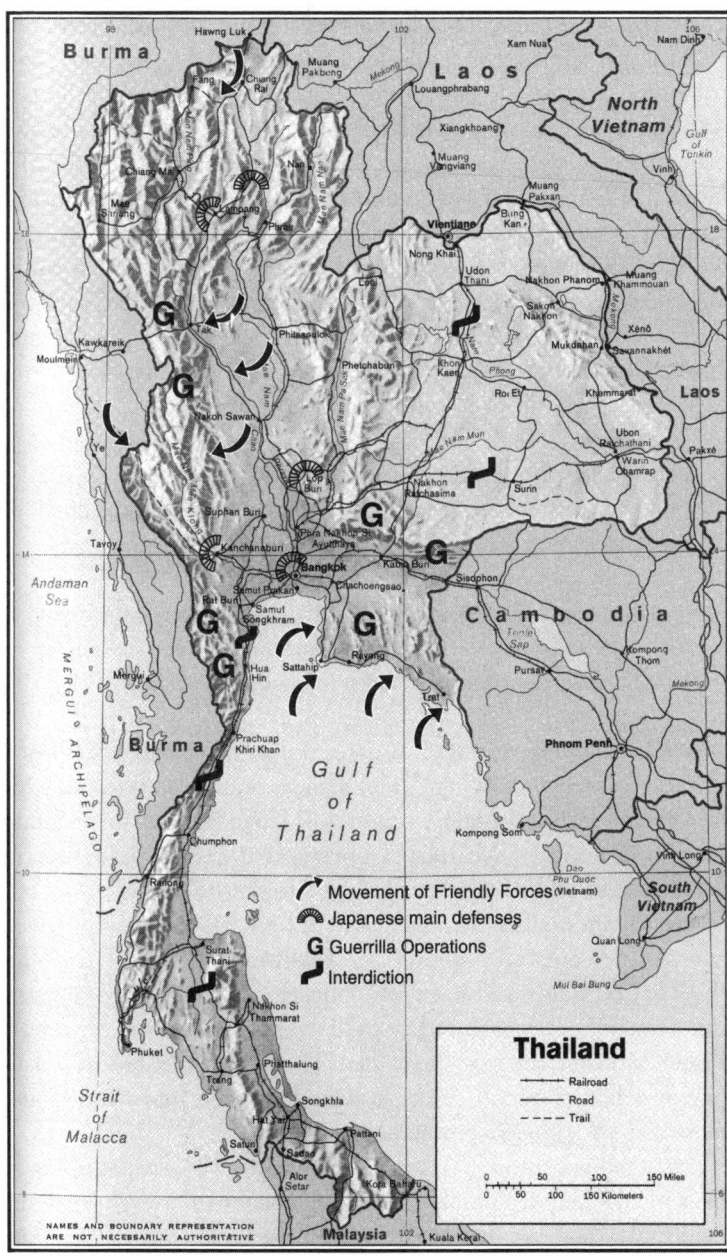

to disarm our troops and police, and declare martial law. . . They knew about the underground, but they did not know its extent."[37] Pridi was apprehensive that his forces would be preempted and prevented from taking part in the offensive against Japan. His view was that it was essential that Thai forces take an active part in any Allied combat operation against the Japanese in Thailand. On the other hand, the Allies were concerned with strategic and tactical goals. The military commander was considerably less concerned with and sensitive to Thai political anxieties. Mountbatten could not afford a premature Thai-Japanese conflict to interfere with the overall long-range plan for military operations to reoccupy Burma, Malaya, and Singapore. Thai eagerness to get into the action was expressed by an underground member after the war:

> Our recruits were so keen on getting at the Japanese that it is a wonder no premature action took place, which might have jeopardized the whole scheme. The plan was to wait until the Japanese were hard-pressed by the allied armies. When word was given by S.E.A.C. [Southeast Asia Command] all the guerrilla units would attack and harass Japanese supply lines in a concentrated effort to render reinforcement or withdrawal of their troops difficult or impossible.[38]

Pridi was most anxious to initiate combat before his forces lost a chance to enter the conflict: "[He] made repeated offers to bring his movement into the open to fight the Japanese, but for military reasons the Allied Military Command urged him to remain underground and he reluctantly agreed to do so.[39]

The Japanese created a major crisis in May 1945 when they levied another in a series of "requests" for Thai funds. While the drain on the Thai economy had been felt almost since the start of the war, this demand for several hundred million baht was particularly severe. Prime Minister Khuang knew that Thailand could not afford to pay, but feared refusal to do so would provide Japan the excuse needed to seize the government.

Pridi radioed the U.S. State Department that Thailand would have to take military action against the Japanese to prevent national bankruptcy and the ouster of the Khuang government. The State

Department, although knowledgeable of the probable impact on the Thai economy, requested that Pridi take no action without coordinating with Lord Mountbatten. They urged Khuang to stall the Japanese and avoid payment for a long as possible.[40]

Pridi reported the increased economic aggression to Lord Mountbatten and insisted that Thailand would not meet the Japanese demands. The urgency of Pridi's message caused consternation in Ceylon. Pridi's economic expertise was unquestioned. If he reported the situation to be that serious, it was indeed critical. Yet the Allies were not militarily prepared to take the offensive from Burma to Thailand, and Lord Mountbatten could not chance a Thai-Japanese military confrontation. Conscious of the sacrifice his guidance would cause Thailand, Mountbatten urged Pridi to exercise his best leadership to keep the resistance movement "under ground" for a few additional months. He made it clear that the Allies would not be able to support a unilateral Thai military action, and he was not yet able to begin the Allied offensive. Mountbatten realized that the Thai resistance was more valuable as an intelligence source than as additional troops for his military forces in Burma.[41]

Lord Mountbatten dispatched Nicol Smith to Washington for briefings at the State Department before sending him to Bangkok as his personal representative to the underground leadership. The State Department's chief of Southeast Asia affairs, Abbot L. Moffet, told Smith:

> The most important thing for you to impress on the Siamese Regent is that he must not make any overt act until Supreme Commander Mountbatten gives the word. The British are planning an attack. Find out from Mountbatten the date they have set for it and persuade Ruth to hold off his uprising to coordinate with that day.[42]

Mountbatten instructed Smith to tell the Thai leader to plan for an Allied attack in November 1945. Smith flew to Thailand with this news. He was met at Phu Khiao by Colonel Thawi Chunlasap, who only recently had returned from India. Thawi escorted the Smith party to Don Mueang air base in a Thai air force plane. They were housed at OSS headquarters in the Suan Kulap Palace.[43] The next day Smith met with the core of the Thai underground: Pridi, Adun, Direk, Thawi Bunyaket, and Thawi Tawetikun. The last-named, director of the bureau of foreign trade, outlined for Smith the seriousness of the economic dilemma facing Thailand.

Smith explained Mountbatten's plans for a November offensive into Thailand and urged Pridi to hold off commitment of the resistance forces until it began. Pridi was not happy, but armed with a tentative date for the Allied offensive, he agreed to comply. He insisted, however, that both the United States and England be fully aware of the economic sacrifice Thailand was making to support the Allies. Smith remained in Thailand until 4 August 1945, acting as the direct link between Lord Mountbatten and the Thai resistance leadership.

The Japanese learned several aspects of the underground plan for an Allied joint operation. Whether by indirect report or espionage, General Nakamura was convinced that the Thai resistance movement was preparing for a major offensive against his forces. At one point the Japanese high command formulated a three-pronged plan to stymie Thai intentions and increase the Japanese hold on the country. The plan called for General Nakamura to tell Prime Minister Khuang that the Japanese knew of Thailand's plans in hope that the resistance operations would stop. Secondly, Nakamura would invite Thai military leaders to a formal dinner party. Those who attended could be captured, while those not in attendance would presumably be underground members who could be apprehended later. In any case the "plot" by the resistance would serve as an excuse to justify disarming the Thai army to neutralize their participation in Allied operations. The third part of the plan called for Nakamura to invite Khuang to make an official visit to Japan. If Khuang refused the invitation it would prove he was unfriendly.[44]

An informant revealed the details of the Japanese plan to Khuang on the day of its implementation. Khuang was thus fortunately prepared to react to Nakamura's sudden visit. Khuang vehemently denied Nakamura's accusations and, in turn, accused Nakamura of plotting to disarm the Thai army and neutralize Thailand's status as a sovereign nation. The confrontation ended in a stalemate. The next day Nakamura invited all Thai officers of the rank of captain and above to attend a dinner at the Japanese military headquarters in Bangkok. Since Khuang felt that a strong Thai turnout would allay Japanese suspicions, he took the risk of arrest and ordered maximum Thai attendance. Over four hundred Thai officers attended the affair. After-dinner speeches by Thai military leaders apparently reassured the Japanese. Khuang also accepted Nakamura's invitation to visit Japan, but successfully delayed the trip.[45]

The German surrender seriously damaged Japan's military position and conversely strengthened the resistance movement's resolve. The Japanese redoubled their suspicions about the loyalty of their Thai "ally," increasing the risk of possible arrest to the underground membership. The movement of Japanese troops forced the resistance to stop operations at bases at Hua Hin and Sam Roi Yot, south of Bangkok. Additionally, the Japanese construction of airstrips and warehouses at Nong Na Plong, Khao Yoi, and Phetchaburi hampered resistance activity. While enemy movement slowed guerrilla training and Allied resupply activity, the Thai informant system reported these new targets to the Allies. This information resulted in several pinpoint bombing raids on the new Japanese facilities.[46]

Thai police and military personnel constructed bunkers and gun emplacements at key points throughout Bangkok. Japanese forces retaliated by building their own fortifications and reinforcing security patrols at key installations. Most underground leaders knew their activities were under increased surveillance. They gave the Japanese commander credit for knowing that the Thais were preparing for a military confrontation.[47]

The underground leadership had good communications with Ceylon and with guerrilla units in the provinces, yet it still needed some signal to alert the thousands of supporters in Bangkok when the time came to start hostilities against the Japanese in the city. An elaborate chain of alert notification procedures relied on a melodramatic but effective visual signal from the underground. For three months, starting in May 1945, Luang Suphachalasai, minister of public health and interior, wore a special civil servant's uniform with oversized buttons on the blouse and a double set of collar insignia. Thai and Japanese alike soon became accustomed to the eccentric appearance of the elderly minister. However, the alert signal for thousands of Bangkok underground cadre was to be the appearance of Luang Suphachalasai in public with *normal* collar insignia.[48]

Mountbatten had promised Pridi to give twenty-four-hour advance notification of the Allied attack. The signal from Luang Suphachalasai would have allowed enough time for disseminating the alert notice. Members of the underground would wear a white armband with blue stripes as a recognition signal.[49]

By mid 1945 the Japanese intelligence system had firm evidence on the location of resistance landing fields throughout Thailand. Their reconnaissance flights had spotted several of the new air fields. Furthermore, the Kempeitai was certain that legitimate Thai air bases were used for resistance operations. Japanese military head-quarters planned a major operation to destroy the secret bases in northeast Thailand and curtail Allied training and communications capabilities. The Twenty-second Division in Laos and a separate battalion from Bangkok were directed to converge on Sakon Nakhon, while the entire Thailand garrison was placed on full alert in case the operation precipitated an uprising by the Thai army.[50]

Nakamura demanded that an immediate joint Thai-Japanese team inspect official air force bases at Phu Khiao and Udon Thani. Khuang had no choice but to comply, but he assigned resistance leaders to the inspection teams. He also stalled, so that resistance forces in these areas could evacuate Allied personnel and equipment. When the inspection team reached Phu Khiao, all guerrilla forces had left, all underground members were gone, and the American team was safely hidden.[51] The Japanese military operation against Sakon Nakhon, scheduled to start on 19 August, never occurred.

VICTORY, POLITICS, AND ALLIED REACTION

The surrender of Japanese forces in Thailand followed the dropping of atomic bombs on Hiroshima and Nagasaki. Thai forces had anticipated the surrender and Japanese troops apparently had planned for it some weeks before the formal end of the war. The

Japanese were still astonished when American officials suddenly appeared in Bangkok and in the provinces on 15 August to represent the Allies until Lord Mountbatten's headquarters could send official representation.

The Thai resistance was disappointed since there was no opportunity to show its military strength in operations against the Japanese. Resistance forces had waited years to fight, so the peaceful end of the war in Thailand chagrined both guerrillas and political leaders. However, no time was lost in initiating the necessary political steps formally to end the war. Prime Minister Khuang immediately annulled the 1942 declarations of war. Pridi prepared a Royal Declaration of Peace that invalidated the two war declarations, stating they were a violation of the Thai constitution and not representative of the will of the people.[52]

The Seri Thai paraded in Bangkok shortly after the arrival of Allied representatives. Political leaders and guerrilla units marched as organized forces with all their weapons, to show the Allies the results of their support. The units needed several hours to pass the reviewing stand on Rajadamnoen Avenue. Since one major reason for an active Thai resistance movement was to secure Allied support in the postwar political settlement, the parade showed conclusively that the Thai had made a significant contribution to the war effort. Resistance leaders told their Allied sponsors that they were depending on the Office of Strategic Services and the Special Operations Executive to support Thailand in the political meetings to follow the war.[53]

The postwar political settlement of Thailand is not germane to this study. The lengthy postwar maneuvering between Thailand, England, and the United States was complex and, at times, acrimonious. American support was critical to Thailand's ability to resist British economic and political demands. Thai resistance was crucial in gaining American support that avoided the imposition by England of harsh economic and political restitutions.

Although the Thai resistance movement did not participate militarily in the defeat of the Japanese, it did succeed in influencing the course of postwar events and in achieving the original political goals set by the resistance leadership.

CHAPTER SEVEN

ANALYSIS AND CONCLUSIONS

The Thai resistance movement during World War II was a unique organization that combined the characteristics of government, political party, and the classic wartime underground. The movement changed in scope and strength as time and events altered the internal situation in the country. While active resistance was generally of low intensity and organization (in contrast with the French Maquis or the Yugoslav partisans), the movement played as significant a role in the history of Thailand as did the French and Yugoslav resistance organizations in their nations.

While the leadership echelon of the resistance was similar to that of a political party, especially after mid 1944, it is clear that its strength and the level of support by the Thais were greater than that of a political party. It is true that many leaders of the Seri Thai were prominent political leaders at the start of the war, while many others began prominent political careers in the postwar era. But it is inaccurate to ascribe postwar political events and individual career developments to the resistance movement as it existed during the war.

Many of the resistance leaders were politically ambitious, but their actions in leading the underground were motivated by genuine patriotism and nationalism. They were alarmed at the Japanese occupation of their country and feared that the Phibun government would endanger Thailand's continued sovereignty.

During the war years the resistance movement adhered to the precepts announced in 1942 by M.R. Seni Pramoj in Washington, D.C. A combination of loyal Thais from all walks of life formed the Seri Thai to restore freedom to the country and to pursue the beginnings of democracy that came with the end of the absolute monarchy in 1932. Membership in the resistance movement spread far beyond the initial circle of Pridi Banomyong's personal loyalists. That resistance leaders were of such disparate personal political loyalties as Pridi, General Adun Adundecharat, and General Chit Mansin Sinatyotharak supports the view that resistance to the Japanese transcended domestic political considerations.

The Thai resistance did not confront the Japanese in traditional forms of guerrilla warfare or high intensity battle. Yet this does not detract from the intent of the resistance movement or invalidate its claim to legitimacy as a major anti-Japanese organization. The resistance movement was primarily organizational and administrative in its activities and political goals because of the absence of a military struggle. But at the end of the war it was fully prepared to enter active combat against the Japanese. Only strong pressure from the Allied command in Ceylon kept Pridi from taking this step long before the Allies were prepared to launch their own offensive in Burma.

The Thai resistance maintained many of the primary characteristics associated with anti-government underground organizations. The leadership was small and maintained strict security. Leadership groups and field elements were compartmented from each other. The leadership recognized early in the war the importance of communications and support from external sources, and emphasized those factors for the duration of the war. They actively sought external support, which was crucial to the success of the resistance movement. Once received, that assistance was used effectively.

The disparate elements of the Thai resistance were assigned appropriate missions. Designated areas of responsibility were within the capabilities of the groups to which they were assigned. Centralized command and control of the movement assured proper coordination of plans and activities both within Thailand and with supporting Allied organizations. In considering the unusual circumstances surrounding the resistance concept in Thailand, the movement was a superb example of a successful underground organization.

INTERNATIONAL IMPLICATIONS OF THE THAI RESISTANCE MOVEMENT

The Thai resistance movement evolved amid unusual international politics. Thailand, as an ally of Japan, declared war on the United States and England. For many reasons the United States did not react to the declaration, although England did. The resulting schism in Allied political policy toward Thailand was at times acrimonious and hampered a concerted Allied effort in Southeast Asia. Significantly, ideals as well as political realities enabled America to support the Thai resistance movement from the start.

In contrast, England's different approach to the Thai resistance delayed official British support. Once given, that support was largely for practical wartime tactical considerations. The Thai resistance leadership recognized the difference in Allied policies toward Thailand and attempted to exploit them to Thailand's advantage. Thai leaders were able to gain the support of both the American government and most of the American people for their plea for postwar political independence. Britain, before World War II the dominant foreign presence in Thailand, saw its influence decline after the war ended. The support of the United States during and after the war played a major role in the marked increase of American influence and presence in Thailand in the postwar era.

Thailand's prewar government acted in what it considered was the country's best interest. At first Prime Minister Phibun was certain that the Axis would win the war. Only after Japan's military fortunes declined did he change his mind. Throughout his time in office Phibun tried to ally Thailand with the winning side. When the Khuang government came to power in 1944 it maintained its overtly friendly relationship with Japan out of necessity. It was some time before the resistance movement had the strength to challenge Japanese forces. Covertly, virtually the entire government structure was integrated into the resistance movement, certainly from mid 1944 onward. This produced a unique situation in which the national government of a belligerent country was in fact the core of that country's resistance movement against its ostensible ally.

THE SERI THAI'S POLITICAL IMPACT

Both Pridi Banomyong and M.R. Seni Pramoj viewed the resistance movement as a means for achieving postwar political goals. Although both men organized their segments of the movement separately, the same goals governed their actions. Popular opinion holds that a resistance movement is created by deeply held beliefs and a spontaneous expression of freedom. The average Thai resistance recruit joined the movement for these reasons. But the resistance leadership held no such illusory beliefs. Although their feelings regarding freedom were sincere, both Seni and Pridi consciously formed the resistance movement as a political tool for future use in retaining Thailand's independence.

Pridi probably would have organized some form of opposition to Phibun under any circumstances, as part of the traditional progression of Thai political history. But the country's position in World War II provided him with a perfect ideological issue that facilitated formation of a massive following and added to his personal power in postwar politics.

The importance of the resistance movement in gaining American support for Thailand is shown in the prominent position the Seri Thai occupies in diplomatic documents. Exchanges between the U.S. State Department and the American embassy in London, as well as direct exchanges between the United States and England, repeatedly mention the resistance movement as a key element in American support of the Thai. In turn, American support was critical for the success of the resistance in organizing a viable movement that could have contributed to an Allied military offensive in Thailand if one had occurred. Now, history has shown the value of the Thai resistance movement in the country's postwar settlement.

REGIONAL COOPERATION

Given the variances in national interests of the Allies in respect to Thailand, their cooperation in the resistance is noteworthy. The Chinese placed innumerable hindrances in front of Allied efforts to organize and support an intelligence-gathering capability through the Thai resistance. The rivalry between American and British intelligence often hampered common efforts. However, when it became clear that operations in Thailand could aid their common war effort, the Allies improved their level of cooperation and coordination.

Thai resistance leaders worked harmoniously with representatives of both England and the United States. Americans were the favored party. The United States enjoyed greater prestige in Thailand by virtue of its faster responses and a closer ideological identity with Thailand's political aspirations. In the final analysis, though, all three countries were able to conduct operations that fostered their respective national interests.

PARTICIPATION AND MEMBERSHIP IN THE RESISTANCE MOVEMENT

The Thai resistance movement was one of the largest of World War II in the sheer size of its membership. All elements of Thai society participated in the movement, including members of the royal family. After Khuang Aphaiwong became prime minister the scope of the movement was enormous. The movement included the liberal X.O. Group circle of leaders, many members of the national and local governments, police and military forces, and thousands of Thais who joined resistance units in all parts of the country.

The geographical spread of the resistance movement in Thailand has been demonstrated. Guerrilla units and underground leadership were organized in most areas of the country and in all major population centers. American or British officers, or Thai agents under their supervision, were stationed in at least forty-two of Thailand's provinces. Major airstrips functioned routinely in the remote areas of Loei and Chaiyaphum provinces and with less regularity in several other areas. Allied seaplanes landed regularly in both the Gulf of Siam and the Andaman Sea. Parachute drops of men and supplies occurred throughout Thailand.

THE RESISTANCE MOVEMENT AND HISTORY

The postwar result of Thai resistance activity is extensive. In general terms, Thailand emerged from World War II with its independence and sovereignty intact. Thailand returned to England and France the colonial territories it had gained from Japan—Burma, Indochina, and Malaya. Some financial compensation was made for Western interests lost in the war. But national sovereignty, the ultimate goal of the resistance movement, was achieved.

The individual histories of the leaders of the resistance movement and its Allied supporters provides a marvelous series of historical vignettes since so many Thai and Allied leaders went on to distinguished careers after the war. The struggle between Pridi and Phibun continued, culminating in Phibun's return to power and Pridi's exile to China and later to France. Many of the leaders in the resistance movement assumed positions of power and influence in postwar Thailand. Some are still active today in Thai commerce, government, and business circles.

Many of the Allied intelligence officers who served in Thailand during World War II established permanent residence in the country and achieved prominence. Probably the best known of these is Jim Thompson. He came to Thailand late in the war and remained in the country for most of his life, where he achieved fame for restoring the Thai silk industry. He disappeared mysteriously from a vacation cottage in Malaysia in the late 1960s. The mystery remains unsolved and has entered the folklore of Southeast Asia. Other former resistance figures who became prominent in Thailand include Alexander MacDonald, who became editor of the leading English-language newspaper, the *Bangkok Post*, and Puay Ungphakon, who achieved prominence in the fields of economics and education. Several Thai agents distinguished themselves in military service.

The Thai resistance movement was responsible in large measure for the emergence of postwar Thailand as an independent nation. It provided the power base of individuals who were to become major Thai leaders. As such, it remains a major benchmark in the history of Southeast Asia.

APPENDIX ONE

OFFICE OF STRATEGIC SERVICES (OSS)
Thailand Operation First Deployment Group, 1943

Thai Name	Nickname Used by OSS
Anon Na Pomphet	Arnold
Anon Siwatthana	Anant
Bunliang Tamthai	Boon
Bunyen Sasirat	Bunny
Bunyong Nikhrothanon	Nick
Chalong Puengtrakun	Charles
Chamrat Follett	Dick
Chamrun Ditsayanan	Kai
Chintamai Amatayakun	Jim
Chok Na Ranong	Charles/Chok
*M.L. Ekachai Kamphu	Ek
Ian Khamphanon	Ian
Karawek Siwichan	Cary
*Karun Kengradomying	Ken
Pao Kham-urai	Phao
Phiset Pattaphong	Pat
Phisut Suthat	Pete
Phon Intharathat	Paul
Sawat Chiaosakun	Sam
Somphong Salayaphong	Sal
Wichian Waiwanon	Victor
M.C. Yuthitsathian Sawatdiwat	John

*Traveled separately to China

AMERICAN OSS PERSONNEL

Captain Frank Gleason
Captain Nicol Smith
Lieutenant Leo Karwaski
Lieutenant Joe Lazarski
Sergeant Tom Lux

From Smith and Clark, *Into Siam, Underground Kingdom*, p. 302; Puay, "Tahan Chuakhrao," pp. 472–473; Wimon, *Free Thai,* pp. 2–3.

APPENDIX TWO

OFFICE OF STRATEGIC SERVICES (OSS)
Thailand Operation Second and Third Deployment Groups, 1944

Second Deployment Group, April 1944

Thai Name	Nickname Used by OSS
Amnuai Phunphiphat	Amnuay
Ayut Itsarasena	Ayus
Bunyong Nikhrothanon	unknown
Chaloem Chittinan	Cal
Chalong Puengtrakun	Charles
*Chanai Rueangsiri	Doctor Ya
Charoen Charoenratchaphak	unknown
Charot Lohasuwan	Los
Kusa Panyarachun	King
Prayun Attachinda	Ray
Sala Thatsanon	Sall
Sit Sawetsila	Sid
Sunthon Suntharakun	unknown
Udom Phattanaphongphanit	Dan
Udomsak Phasawanit	Don

Third Deployment Group (Direct OSS Recruits)

Luang Atphisankit	unknown
Bunloet Kasemsuwan	unknown
Chuea Hunchamlong	Chua

From Wimon, *Free Thai,* p. 5.

APPENDIX THREE

SPECIAL OPERATIONS EXECUTIVE (SOE)
Thailand Operation First Deployment Group, 1943

Thai Name	Nickname Used by SOE
Arun Sonthet	Kai Fa
Bunphop Phamonsing	Pope
Bunsong Phuengsunthon	Chai
M.L. Chirayu Nopphawong	unknown
M.C. Chiridanai Kitiyakon	Ri
Chunkheng (Phatphong) Rinthakun	Phong
Kamhaeng Phalangkun	Lore
M.C. Karawik Chakraphan	Ratsami
M.R. Kitinatda Kitiyakon	unknown
Klin Thep-hatsadin Na Ayutthaya	unknown
M.C. Kokasat Sawatdiwat	unknown
Krit Totsayanon	Khong
Pat Pathamasathan	Na
Luang Phatharawathi	unknown
M.C. Phisadet Ratchani	Man
Phunphoem Krairoek	Poon
Prachit Kangsanon	Kay
Praphot Paorohit	Nun
Praphruet Na Nakhon	Lek
Prasoet Pathummanon	Pao
Prathan Premkamon	Daeng
Prem Buri	Dee
Puay Ungphakon	Khem
Rachit Buri, M.D.	Kham
Samran Wannaphruek	Kheng
Sano Ninkhamhaeng	Chieu
Sawang Samkoset	unknown
Sawat Sisuk	Raven
Somchit Yotsunthon	unknown
M.C. Suphasawatwongsanit Sawatdiwat	Major Arun

Thana Potsayanon	Khon
Thep Semthiti	Noo/Na
Thot Phanthumsen	Bun
To Bunnak	unknown
Wattana Chitwari	Thuan
Wiwat Na Pomphet	unknown
Yimyon Taesuchi	unknown

From Thawi Bunyaket, *Thailand and World War II*, pp. 388–389; Gilchrist, *Bangkok Top Secret*, p. 206.

APPENDIX FOUR

DEPLOYMENT OF THAI OSS AND FORCE 136 AGENTS IN THE THAI RESISTANCE MOVEMENT

Name	Nickname	Date and Place Entered Thailand	Sponsorship	Deployment
Amnuai Phonphipat	Amnuay	Nov 44, Chiang Mai	OSS	Sakon Nakhon
Anon Na Pomphet	Arnold	Nov 44, Kratan Is.	OSS	Chonburi
Arun Sonthet	Kai Fa	Mar 45, unknown	Force 136	Tak
Ayut Itsarasena	Ayus	Mar 45, Chiang Rai	OSS	Chiang Rai
Bunliang Tamthai	Boon	unknown	OSS	unknown
Bunmak Thetsabut	Ben	Sept 44, Phrae	OSS	Bangkok; Hua Hin
Bunrot Binthasan	Ben	Did not enter	OSS	Szemao
Bunsong Phuengsunthon	Chai	Mar 45,* Chan Is.	Force 136	Ranong
Bunyen Sasirat	Bunny	Aug 44, Chiang Rai	OSS	Nakhon Si Thammarat
Bunyong Nikhrothanon	Nick	unknown	OSS	unknown
Chaloem Chittinan	Cal	Nov 44, Chiang Mai	OSS	captured
Chalong Puengtrakul	Charles	Feb 45, Sakon Nakhon	OSS	Sakon Nakhon
Chamrat Follett	Dick	unknown	OSS	remained in Ceylon
Chamrun Ditsayanan	Kai	unknown	OSS	unknown
Chanai Rueangsiri	Dr. Ya	Mar 45, Bangkok	OSS	Bangkok; Phetchaburi

Name	Nickname	Date and Place Entered Thailand	Sponsorship	Deployment
Charoen Wattanaphanit	Carl	Feb 45, Bangkok	OSS	Phu Khiao
Charot Lohasuwan	Los	Mar 45,* unknown	OSS	Phrae
Chintamai Amatayakun	Jim	unknown	OSS	remained in Ceylon
M.C. Chiridanai Kitiyakon	Ri/Thong	unknown	Force 136	unknown location in S. Thailand
Chok Na Ranong	Chok	unknown	OSS	remained in Ceylon
Chuea Hunchamlong	Chua	Mar 45,* Chan Is.	OSS	Chumphon
Chun Silasuwan	Charlie	Mar 45,* unknown	OSS	Udon Thani
Chunkheng Rinthakun	Phong	Apr 44, Chainat	Force 136	Bangkok
Ekachai Kamphu	Ek	May 45, Chonburi	OSS	Bangkok
Ian Khamphanon	Ian	Apr 44, Chiang Rai	OSS	Khlong Phai; Ang Thong
Kamhaeng Phalangkun	Lore	Mar 45,* unknown	Force 136	Bangkok
Karawek Siwichan	Cary	Apr 44, Chiang Rai	OSS	killed by Thai police
M.C. Karawik Chakraphan	Ratsami	Mar 45, unknown	Force 136	Tak
Karun Kengradomying	Ken	Apr 44, Chiang Rai	OSS	Bangkok; Szemao; Ubon
Klin Thep-hatsadin Na Ayutthaya	Khao	unknown	Force 136	remained in Ceylon
Krit Totsayanon	Khong	Sept 44, Hua Hin	OSS	Bangkok; Sakon Nakhon
Kusa Panyarachun	King	Nov 44, Kratan Is.	OSS	captured
Nithiphat Chanichan	Nick	unknown	OSS	Nakhon Nayok
Pao Kham-urai	Pao	Aug 44, Chiang Rai	OSS	Bangkok; Phetchaburi
Pat Pathomsathan	Na	Mar 45, unknown	Force 136	Tak
M.C. Phisadet Ratchani	Man	Apr 45, Phuket	Force 136	Phuket
Phiset Pattaphong	Pat	unknown	OSS	Khon Kaen; Bangkok

143

Name	Nickname	Date and Place Entered Thailand	Sponsorship	Deployment
Prasut Suthat	Pete	Aug 44, Chiang Rai	OSS	Bangkok; Prachinburi
Phon Intharathat	Paul	May 44, Phrae	OSS	Phitsanulok; Bangkok
Phunphoem Krairoek	Poon	Mar 45,* Bangkok	OSS	Bangkok
Prachit Kangsanon	Kay	May 45, unknown	Force 136	Bangkok
Praphot Poorohit	Noon	Dec 44, Nakhon Sawan	Force 136	Phu Kradung
Praphruet Na Nakhon	Lek	Mar 45,* unknown	Force 136	Bangkok
Prasoet Pathumanon	Pao	Sept 44, Hua Hin	OSS	Bangkok
Prathan Premkamon	Daeng	Apr 44, Chainat	Force 136	Bangkok
Prayun Attachinda	Ray	Mar 45,* unknown	OSS	Sawankolok
Prem Buri	Di	Apr 44, Chainat	Force 136	Bangkok; Surat Thani
Puay Ungphakon	Khem	Apr 44, Chainat	Force 136	Bangkok; Ceylon; UK; Bangkok
Rachit Buri	Kham	Apr 44, Chainat	Force 136	Bangkok; Yala
Sala Thotsanon	Sall	May 45, Chonburi	OSS	Bangkok; Khlong Phai
Samran Wannaphruek	Khaeng	Apr 44, Chainat	Force 136	Bangkok; Surat Thani
Sano Ninkhamhaeng	Chieu	Dec 44, Nakhon Sawan	Force 136	Phu Kradung
Sawat Chiaosakun	Sam	Aug 44, Chiang Rai	OSS	Khlong Phai
Sawat Sisuk	Raven	Apr 44, Chainat	Force 136	Bangkok
Sit Sawetsila	Siri	Nov 44, Chiang Mai	OSS	captured
Somchit Kangsanon	Sonny	Mar 45, Kanchanaburi	OSS	Kanchanaburi
Somphong Sanlayaphong	Sal	Apr 44, Chiang Rai	OSS	killed by Thai police
Sunthon Khanthalaksana	Sun	Mar 45,* Chan Is.	OSS	Ranong

144

Name	Nickname	Date and Place Entered Thailand	Sponsorship	Deployment
M.C. Suphasawatdiwongsanit Sawatdiwat	Major Arun	Jan 45, Bangkok	Force 136	Bangkok; Ceylon; Bangkok; Tak; Surat Thani
Thana Potsayanon	Kon	Apr 44, Chainat	Force 136	Bangkok; Yala
Thep Semthiti	Na	Dec 44, Nakhon Sawan	Force 136	Phu Kradung
Thot Phanthumsen	Bun	Mar 45, unknown	Force 136	Tak
Udom Pattanaphongphanit	Dan	unknown	OSS	unknown
Udomsak Phasawanit	Don	Nov 44, Chiang Mai	OSS	captured
Wattana Chitwari	Thuan	Apr 45, Phuket	Force 136	Phuket
Wichian Waiwanon	Victor	unknown	OSS	Khon Kaen
Wimon Wiriyawit	Wyman	Sept 44, Phrae	OSS	Bangkok; Nakhon Ratchasima
M.C. Yuthitsathian Sawatdiwat	John	May 45, Phu Khiao	OSS	Phu Khiao

Asterisk (*) indicates estimated month of infiltration into Thailand.
Collected from multiple sources, listed in bibliography.

APPENDIX FIVE

ROSTER OF THAI PARTICIPANTS IN THE THAI RESISTANCE MOVEMENT *

Name	Transliteration	Familiar Spelling	Affiliation
กนฺตีรุ์ สุภมงคล	Konthi Suphamongkhon		Liaison Officer, Ceylon
กระจ่าง ผลเพิ่ม	Krachang Phonphoem		Thai Army/China Contact
กรี้ เดชาติวงศ์	Kri Dechatiwong		X.O. Group
กฤษณ์ โตษยานนท์	Krit Totsayanon		Force 136
กลิ่น เทพหัสดิน ณ อยุธยา	Klin Thep-hatsadin Na Ayutthaya		Force 136
ม.จ. กอกสัตร์ สวัสดิวัตน์	M.C. Kokasat Sawatdiwat	Koksatri Svasti	Force 136
การุณ เกงระดมยิ่ง	Karun Kengradomying		OSS
ม.จ. การวิก จักรพันธุ์	M.C. Karawik Chakraphan	Karawik Chakrabandhu	Force 136
การวก ศิริวิจารณ์	Karawek Siwichan		OSS
กำแหง พลางกูร	Kamhaeng Phalangkun		Force 136
ม.ร.ว. กิตินัดดา กิติยากร	M.R. Kitinatda Kitiyakon	Kitinadda Kitiyakara	Force 136
กุศะ ปันยารชุน	Kusa Panyarachun	Kusa Panyarajun	OSS
โกเมศ เครือตรัชู	Komet Khrueatrachu		OSS
ม.ล. ขาบ กุญชร	M.L. Khap Kunchon	Khap Kunjara	OSS
ขุนพิชัยมนตรี	Khun Phichaimontri		Underground

146

Name	Transliteration	Familiar Spelling	Affiliation
ควง อภัยวงศ์	Khuang Aphaiwong	Khuang Aphaiwongse	Underground
โชค ณ ระนอง	Chok Na Ranong		OSS
จรูญ สุนแสง	Charun Sunsaeng		Underground
จำกัด พลางกูร	Chamkat Phalangkun	Chamkat Plangkura	Underground
จำรัส ฟอลเลต	Chamrat Follet		OSS
จำรูญ ดิษยะนันท์	Chamrun Ditsayanan		OSS
จำลอง ดาวเรือง	Chamlong Daorueang		Underground
จินตมัย อมาตยกุล	Chintamai Amatayakun	Chintamai Amatyakul	OSS
จิระ วิชิตสงคราม	Chira Wichitsongkhram		Thai Army
ม.ล. จิรายุ นพวงศ์	M.L. Chirayu Nopphawong	Jirayu Naphawongse	Force 136
ม.จ. จิรีดนัย กิติยากร	M.C. Chiridanai Kitiyakon	Chiridanai Kitiyakara	Force 136
จุนเคง (พัฒนพงษ์) รินทกุล	Chunkheng Phatphong Rinthakun		Force 136
เจริญ เจริญรัชตภาคย์	Charoen Charoenratchattaphak		OSS
เจริญ วัฒนะพานิช	Charoen Watthanaphanit		OSS
ฉลอย ฉัยทัต	Chaloei Chaithat		Underground
ฉลอง ปึงตระกูล	Chalong Puengtrakun		OSS
เฉลิม จิตตินันท์	Chaloem Chittinan		OSS
โฉน เรืองศิริ	Chanai Rueangsiri		OSS
ฉาญ บุนนาค	Chan Bunnak	Chan Bunnag	Underground

Name	Transliteration	Familiar Spelling	Affiliation
ชาติ นักรบ	Chat Nakrop		Thai Army
ชโล อินทรอัมพร	Chalo Inthara-amphon		Thai Army
ชโรจน์ โลหะสุวรรณ	Charot Lohasuwan		OSS
ชิต มั่นศิลป์ สินาถโยธารักษ์	Chit Mansin Sinatyotharak		Thai Army
ชุน ศิลสุวรรณ์	Chun Silasuwan		OSS
ฉัน สุวันทับ	Chan Suwanthap		Underground
เฉียบ (ไชยสงค์) อัมพุนันท์	Chiap (Chaisong) Amphunan		Underground/Police
เชื้อ หุ่นจำลอง	Chuea Hunchamlong		OSS
เชาว์ คลิ่งสัมฤทธิ์	Chao Khlaisamrit		Underground/Police
เชาวงศ์ แสนสิริพันธ์	Chaowong Saensiriphan		Underground
เดือน บุนนาค	Duean Bunnak	Duan Bunnag	Underground
หลวงดิฐฐการภักดี	Luang Dithakan Phakdi		Seri Thai—U.S.
ดิเรก ชัยนาม	Direk Chaiyanam	Direk Jayanama	Underground
เดช เดชปรดียุทธ	Det Detpradiyuth		China Contact
เดช สนิทวงศ์	Det Sanitwong	Dej Snidvong	Underground
เดชา บุญยะคุปต์	Decha Bunyakhup		China Contact
แดง คุณะดิลก	Daeng Khunadilok		Underground
เตียง ศิริขันธ์	Tiang Sirikhan		Underground
โต บุนนาค	To Bunnak	To Bunnag	Force 136

148

Name	Transliteration	Familiar Spelling	Affiliation
กนิษฐ์ คอมันตร์	Thanat Khoman		Underground—U.S.
ถวิล อุดล	Thawin Udon		Underground
ทวี จุลละทรัพย์	Thawi Chunlasap		Thai Air Force
ทวี ตะเวทิกุล	Thawi Tawetikun		Underground
ทวี ตุลวรรธนะ	Thawi Tunwaranthana		China Contact
ทวี บุณยเกตุ	Thawi Bunyaket		Underground
ทอง กันทาธรรม	Thong Kanthatham		Underground
ทองปลาว ชลภูมิ	Thongplao Chonaphum		Underground
ทศ พันธุมเสน	Thot Phanthumsen		Force 136
ทองอินทร์ ภูริพัฒน์	Thong-in Phuriphat		Underground
เทพ เสมะติติ	Thep Semthiti		Force 136
ธนา โปษยานนท์	Thana Posayanon		Force 136
ธานี สาทรกิจ	Thani Sathonkit		China Contact
นิธิพัฒน์ ชาลีจันทร์	Nithiphat Chalichan	Nithiphat Jalichandra	OSS
เนตร เขมะโยธิน	Net Khemayothin		Underground
บรรจง ชิพเพ็นสุข	Banchong Chippensuk		Underground/Police
หลวงบรรณกรโกวิท	Luang Bannakhon Kowit		Underground
บุญพบ ภมรสิงห์	Bunphop Phamonsing		Force 136
บุญมาก เทศบุตร	Bunmak Thetsabut		OSS

149

Name	Transliteration	Familiar Spelling	Affiliation
บุญยง นิโครธานนท์	Bunyong Nikhrothanon		OSS
บุญเย็น ศะสิรัตน์	Bunyen Sasirat		OSS
บุญรอด บิณฑสันต์	Bunrot Binthasan		OSS
บุญเลิศ เกษมสุวรรณ	Bunloet Kasemsuwan		Force 136
บุญเลี้ยง ตามไท	Bunliang Tamthai		OSS
บุญส่ง พึงสุนทร	Bunsong Phuengsunthon		Force 136
ป๋วย อึ๊งภากรณ์	Puai Uengphakon	Puay Ungphakorn	Force 136
ปาพร์ ปัทมสถาน	Pat Pathamasathan		Force 136
ประจิตร กังศานนท์	Prachit Kangsanon		Force 136
ประฐาน เปรมกมล	Prathan Premkamon		Force 136
ประพฤทธิ์ ณ นคร	Praphruet Na Nakhon		Force 136
ประโพธิ เปาโรหิต	Praphot Paorohit		Force 136
ประยูร อรรถจินดา	Prayun Attachinda	Prayoon Arthachinta	OSS
	Prasat Suwannasombun		Underground/Police
ประสิทธิ์ กีรกระจินดา	Prasit Kirakrachinda		Underground
ประเสริฐ ปทุมานนท์	Prasoet Pathummanon		Force 136
ปรีดี พนมยงค์	Pridi Phanomyong	Pridi Banomyong	Seri Thai—Thailand
เปรม บุรี	Prem Buri		Force 136
แปลก พิบูลสงคราม	Plaek Phibunsongkhram	Plaek Phibulsongkram	Prime Minister

Name	Transliteration	Familiar Spelling	Affiliation
เปา ฟ้าฦไร	Pao Kham-urai		OSS
ผึ้ง ศรีจันทร์	Phueng Sichan	Phung Srichand	Underground
พะเยิม จันทะรักคะ	Phayom Chantarakha		Police
พัน นาวาวิจิตร	Phan Nawawichit	Phan Navavichit	X.O. Group
พิเศษ ปัทมะพงษ์	Phiset Pattaphong		OSS
พิสุทธิ์ สุทัศน์ ณ อยุธยา	Phisut Suthat Na Ayutthaya		OSS
พูนเพิ่ม ไกรฤกษ์	Phunphoem Krairoek	Poonpeom Krairiksh	OSS
โผน อินทรารัตน์	Phon Intharathat		OSS
หลวงภัทรวาที	Luang Phatharawathi		Force 136
ม.จ.พิสเดช รัชนี	M.C. Phisadet Ratchani		Force 136
รชิต บุรี	Rachit Buri	Rajit Buri	Force 136
มณี สาณะเสน	Mani Sanasen		Seri Thai—U.K.
ยล สมานนท์	Yon Samanon		Underground
ยิมยอ แต้สุจิ	Yimyon Taesuchi		Force 136
ม.จ.ยุธิษเฐียร สวัสดิวัตน์	M.C. Yutthitsathian Sawatdiwat	Yuthisthira Svasti	OSS
วัฒนา จิตรวรี	Watthana Chitwari		Force 136
หลวงวิจิตรวาทการ	Luang Wichit Wathakan	Vichitr Vadakarn	Phibul Government
วิจิตร ลุลิตานนท์	Wichit Lulitanon	Vichit Lulitananda	Underground
วิเชียร วายวานนท์	Wichian Waiwanon		OSS

Name	Transliteration	Familiar Spelling	Affiliation
วิมล วิริยะวิทย์	Wimon Wiriyawit		OSS
หลวงวิรัชวัฒน์โยธิน	Luang Wirawatyothin		Thai Army
วิวรรธน์ ณ ป้อมเพชร	Wiwat Na Pomphet	Vivat Na Pombejra	Force 136
หลวงสุภาชลาศัย	Luang Suphachalasai		X.O. Group
ม.จ. ศุภสวัสดิ์วงศ์สนิท สวัสดิวัตน์	M.C. Suphasawatwongsanit Sawatdiwat Subha Svasti		Force 136
สงวน ตุลารักษ์	Sa-nguan Tularak		Underground
สมจิต ยศสุนทร	Somchit Yotsunthon		Force 136
สมจิตต์ กังสานนท์	Somchit Kangsanon		OSS
สมพงษ์ สัลยาพงษ์	Somphong Sanlayaphong		OSS
สมาน วีระวิทยะ	Saman Wirawaithaya	Saman Viravidhya	China Contact
สละ ทศานนท์	Sala Thotsanon		OSS
สวัสดิ์ ไกรฤกษ์	Sawat Kraireok	Sawat Krairiksh	Underground
สวัสดิ์ เชียวสกุล	Sawat Chiaosakun		OSS
สวัสดิ์ ศรีสุข	Sawat Sisuk	Sawat Srisuk	Force 136
สว่าง สามโกเศศ	Sawang Samkoset		Force 136
สะพรั่ง เทพหัสดิน	Saphrang Thep-hatsadin		Underground
สังวรณ์ สุวรรณชีพ	Sangwon Suwanchip		Thai Navy
สังวรณ์ ยุทธกิจ	Sangwon Yuthakit		X.O. Group
สำราญ วรรณพฤกษ์	Samran Wannaphruek		Force 136

Name	Transliteration	Familiar Spelling	Affiliation
สำเริง เนตรายน	Samroeng Nettrayon		Thai Army
สิทธิ เศวตศิลา	Sit Sawetsila	Siddhi Savetsila	OSS
สุนทร คันธลักษณะ	Sunthon Khanthalaksana		OSS
สุนทร สุนทรากุร	Sunthon Suntharakun		OSS
ม.ร.ว.เสนีย์ ปราโมช	M.R. Seni Pramot	Seni Pramoj	Seri Thai—U.S.
แสวง ณ พัทลุง	Sawaeng Na Phatthalung		Thai Army
แสวง ทัพกลุล	Sawaeng Thapphasut		China Contact
เสนาะ นิลกำแหง	Sano Ninkamhaeng	Sanoh Nilkamhaeng	Force 136
เสนาะ ตันบุญยืน	Sano Tanbunyuen	Sanoh Tanbunyuen	Seri Thai—U.K.
หะริน หงสกุล	Harin Hongsakun		Underground
หาญ สงคราม	Han Songkhram		Thai Army
ใหญ่ ศวิตชาติ	Yai Sawitchat		Underground
อนันต์ จินตกานนท์	Anan Chintokanon		Force 136
อรุณ สรเทศน์	Arun Sonthet		Underground
อาจ ณ บางช้าง	At Na Bangchang		China Contact
หลวงอาจพิศาลคดี	Luang Atphisankit		Force 136
หลวงอดุลย์ อดุลยเดชจรัส	Luang Adun Adundecharat		Underground
อานนท์ ณ ป้อมเพชร	Anon Na Pomphet	Anon Na Pombejra	OSS
อานนท์ ศิวัธนะ	Anon Siwatthana		OSS

153

Name	Transliteration	Familiar Spelling	Affiliation
อยุธ อิศรเสนา	Ayut Itsarasena	Ayus Isarasena	OSS
อำนวย พูนพิพัฒน์	Amnuai Phunphiphat		OSS
อุดม บุญประกอบ	Udom Bunyaprakop		Underground
อุดม ภู่พัฒน์	Udom Phuphat		OSS
อุดม พัฒนพงษ์พานิช	Udom Phatthanaphongphanit		OSS
อุดมศักดิ์ ภาสวนิช	Udomsak Phasawanit		OSS
น.ต. เอกชัย กัมภู	Ekachai Kamphu	Ekachai Kambhu	OSS
เอกศักดิ์ ประพันธโยธิน	Ekasak Praphanotyothin		Underground
เอียน ธัมพานนท์	Ian Khamphanon		OSS

*All Thai citizens who were active in the resistance movement and whose names were mentioned in available sources are listed here. While most prominent members of the resistance are believed to be included in this roster, it is not intended to be a comprehensive listing. The author apologizes for any errors in the Thai spelling and transliteration.

NOTES

AUTHOR'S INTRODUCTION

1 . U.S. Department of the Army, Field Manual 31–21: Special Forces Operations, U.S. Army Doctrine, 20 December 1974. Washington, D.C.: Headquarters Department of the Army, 1974, pp. 3–21.

CHAPTER ONE: POLITICAL AND MILITARY DEVELOPMENTS LEADING TO WORLD WAR II

1. Frank C. Darling, *Thailand and the United States* (Washington, D.C.: Public Affairs Press, 1965), pp. 30–32.

2. Donald E. Nuechterlein, *Thailand and the Struggle for Southeast Asia* (Ithaca, N.Y.: Cornell University Press), pp. 43–44.

2. Darling, loc. cit.

3. M.R. Seni Pramoj, "Relationship Between Thailand and the U.S.A. During the Second World War," a lecture delivered at Chulalongkorn University, Bangkok, on 17 August 1946, contained in a private printing of M.R. Seni's works, pp. 18–19.

4. Fascinating and detailed accounts of this topic are reported in a Thai language book, Direk Chaiyanam, *Thai Kap Songkhram Lok Khrang Thi Song* [Thailand and World War II] (Bangkok: Prae Pittaya Press, 1966).

5. Seni, op. cit., p. 8.

6. James V. Martin Jr., "Thai-American Relations in World War II," *Journal of Asian Studies* 21 (August 1963), p. 459.

7. Ibid.

8. U.S. Department of the Army, *Thailand Operations Record, Japanese Monograph #177* (Tokyo: Headquarters Army Forces Far East, 1953), pp. 4–7.

9. Charoon Kuwanon, *Chiwit Kan To Su Khong Chomphon P. Phibunsongkhram* [The Fighting Life of Marshal P. Phibunsongkhram] (Bangkok: Akson Charoenthat Press, 1953), p. 174.

10. Thawi Bunyaket, *Thai Kap Songkhram Lok Khrang Thi Song* [Thailand and World War II], published as an appendix to Direk Chaiyanam's work of the same name, 1966, pp. 349–355.

11. Colonel S. Phichet, "Siam in World War II, A Description of the Japanese Invasion of Siam and the Effort of the People in Resistance Activities," an unpublished paper presented to the Regular course of the U.S. Army Command and General Staff College, Fort Leavenworth, Kans., 1947, p. 5.

12. Charoon, op. cit., p. 162.

13. Ibid.

14. Charoon, op. cit., pp. 158–161.

15. Thawi Bunyaket, loc.cit.

16. Phichet, op. cit., p. 41.

17. H. C. Quaritch-Wales, "Thailand—Key to the Coming Attack on Japan," *Asia and the Americas* 42 (September 1942), p. 529.

18. Wendell Blanchard, et. al., *Thailand, Its People, Its Society, Its Culture* (New Haven, Conn.: Human Relations Area Files, Inc., 1958), p. 37.

19. Air Chief Marshal Thawi Chunlasap, *Chat Yu Nua Sing Dai* [My Country Above All] (privately published in Bangkok, 1974), pp. 47–48.

20. Thawi Bunyaket, loc. cit.

21. Ibid.

22. U.S. Army, *Thailand Operations Record*, loc. cit.

23. Luang Wichit Wathakan, written in 1947 in *Behind the Declaration of War*, a privately published edition of Wichit's works translated into English (Bangkok, 1967), p. 47.

24. U.S. Army, loc. cit.

25. Wichit, op. cit., p. 55.

26. Ibid., pp. 52–55.

27. Thawi Bunyaket, op.cit. pp. 360–362.

28. Brigadier General M.L. Manich Jumsai, *History of Anglo-Thai Relations* (Bangkok: Chalermnit Press, 1970), p. 261.

29. Brigadier General M.L. Manich Jumsai, *History of Anglo-Thai Relations* (Bangkok: Chalermnit Press, 1970), p. 261.

CHAPTER TWO: FORMATION OF THE THAI RESISTANCE MOVEMENT

1. Blanchard, op. cit., p. 131.
2. Direk, op. cit., p. 319.
3. Sir Andrew Gilchrist, *Bangkok Top Secret* (London: Hutchinson Publishers, 1970), p. 19.
4. Margaret Landon, "Thailand Under the Japanese," *Asia and the Americas* 44 (September 1944), p. 389.
5. Malai Chuphanit (pseudonym Chanthana), *X. O. Group* (Bangkok: Kao Na Printers, 1964), p. 25.
6. Ibid., p. 44.
7. Nuechterlein, op. cit., p. 45.
8. Ibid., pp. 29–31.
9. M.C. Karawik Chakrabandhu, "Force 136 and the Siamese Resistance Movement," *Asiatic Review* 43 (April 1947), pp. 168–169.
10. Landon, loc. cit.
11. Malai, op. cit., pp. 66–69.
12. Ibid., p. 43.
13. Quaritch-Wales, op. cit., p. 530.
14. Landon, op. cit. p. 390.
15. Seni, op. cit., pp. 26–27.
16. Malai, op. cit., pp. 72–73.
17. Darling, op. cit., p. 34.
18. Walter Fitzmaurice, "Thailand, Ally in Secret, Snooped Under Japs' Noses," *Newsweek* 26 (3 September 1945), p. 26.
19. Seni, manuscript of a speech given 17 August 1946, unpaged.
20. Nai Samrej (a pseudonym of an unidentified senior Thai official), "That Thailand May Be Free," *Asia and the America* 45 (February 1945), pp. 94–95.
21. Seni, loc. cit.
22. Samrej, loc. cit.
23. Wimon Wiriyawit, *Free Thai* (Bangkok: White Lotus Press, 1997), pp. 1–2.
24. Darling, op. cit., p. 35.
25. Darling, op. cit., p. 35.
26. Puay Ungphakon, *Thahan Chuakhrao* [Temporary Soldier], an appendix to Direk Chaiyanam's *Thailand and World War II* (cited above), p. 391.
27. Puay, ibid., pp. 384–386.

28. Wilasuang Phongsabutr, *Prawatisat Thai* [History of Thailand] (Bangkok: Thai Wattana Printing Company, Inc., 1976), p. 354.

29. For simplicity, this name is used throughout this book.

30. R. Harris Smith, *OSS: The Secret History of America's First Central Intelligence Agency* (Berkeley, Calif.: University of California Press, 1972), p. 296.

31. Gilchrist, op. cit., pp. 29–30.

CHAPTER THREE: THE RESISTANCE GROUPS STRUGGLE TO ACHIEVE CONTACT, 1942–1943

1. Nicol Smith and Blake Clark, *Into Siam, Underground Kingdom* (New York: Bobbs Merrill Company, 1945), p. 16.

2. Ibid., p. 19.

3. Ibid., p. 18; Wimon, op. cit., p. 78.

4. Wimon, op. cit., p. 3.

5. Ibid., pp. 79–80.

6. U.S. War Department, *War Report: Office of Strategic Services (OSS), Volume 2 (Operations)* (Washington, D.C.: Government Printing Office, 1949), p. 416 and p. 438.

7. See Vice Admiral Milton E. Miles, *A Different Kind of War* (Garden City, N.Y.: Doubleday, 1967), for an excellent account of the intrigues that surrounded Allied relationships in China.

8. Smith and Clark, op. cit., pp. 71–72.

9. U.S. War Department, loc. cit.

10. Ibid., p. 393.

11. Puay, op. cit., pp. 392–394.

12. Gilchrist, loc. cit.

13. Karawik, loc. cit.

14. Gilchrist, op. cit., p. 41.

15. Ibid., p. 33.

16. Chamkat Palangkun, *Free Thai Movement*, a report prepared for transmission to the OSS, 1943, p. 1.

17. Malai, loc. cit.

18. Pridi Banomyong, speech in Bangkok on 26 September 1945, reported to OSS in OSS Memorandum B-27 dated 6 October 1945, U.S. National Archives Document Number XL24262.

19. U.S. Office of Strategic Services, *Political Aspects of an Allied Occu-*

pation of Thailand, Research & Analysis Document Number 2114, dated 14 July 1944, p. 91.

20. Martin, op. cit., p. 462.

21. Malai, op. cit., pp. 56–57.

22. Smith and Clark, op. cit., p. 233.

23. Joseph A. Loftus, "Secret Thai Role in War Detailed," *New York Times*, 9 September 1945, Section II, p. 2.

24. Fitzmaurice, loc. cit.

25. Thawi Bunyaket, op. cit., p. 367.

26. U.S. Office of Strategic Services, *Escape of Allied Airmen from the Kra Isthmus*, OSS Memorandum Number K-90 dated 21 April 1945, U.S. National Archives Document Number 126742.

27. Malai, op. cit., pp. 57–58.

28. Richard M. Kelly, "Mission to Bangkok," *Blue Book*, December 1946, pp. 88–99.

29. Malai, op. cit., pp. 40–41.

30. Ibid., pp. 77 *supra.*

31. Ibid., p. 131.

32. Ibid., p. 159.

33. Ibid., pp. 144–146.

34. Smith and Clark, op. cit., pp. 90–91.

35. Malai, op. cit., p. 135.

36. Ibid., pp. 157–158.

37. Smith, op. cit., p. 306.

38. General Net Khemayothin, *Ngan Tai Din Khong Pan Ek Yothi* [The Underground Work of Colonel Yothi] (Bangkok: Fuang Akson Press, 1967), pp. 8–11 (cited as "Work" in future footnotes).

39. General Net Khemayothin, *Chiwit Khong Naiphon* [A General's Life] (Bangkok: Fuang Akson Press, 1967), p. 263 (cited as "Life" in later footnotes).

40. Net, *Life*, pp. 304–322 contains detailed accounts of this meeting.

41. Net, *Work*, op. cit., pp. 387–393.

42. U.S. War Department, op. cit., p. 359.

43. Net, *Life*, loc. cit.

44. Ibid., pp. 335–341.

45. Jayanta Kumar Ray, *Portraits of Thai Politics* (New Delhi: Orient Longman, Ltd., 1972).

46. Ibid., p. 207.

47. Ibid., p. 203.

48. Net, *Work*, op. cit., pp. 16–18.
49. Ibid., p. 151.
50. Nuechterlein, op. cit., p. 46.

CHAPTER FOUR: INFILTRATION INTO THAILAND, 1943–1944

1. Smith and Clark, op. cit., p. 107.
2. Ibid., pp. 128–129.
3. Net, *Work*, op. cit., pp. 70–71.
4. Ibid.
5. Malai, op. cit., pp. 257–258.
6. Smith and Clark, op. cit., pp. 182–183.
7. Gilchrist, op. cit., pp. 44–45.
8. Ibid., pp. 41–43.
9. Ibid., pp. 45–47.
10. Puay, op. cit., pp. 401–415.
11. Gilchrist, op. cit., p. 61.
12. Ibid., p. 50.
13. Puay, op. cit., pp. 424–425.
14. Ibid.
15. Ibid.
16. Loftus, loc. cit.
17. Wimon, op. cit., pp. 8–9.
18. U.S. War Department, op. cit., p. 407.
19. Wimon, op. cit., pp. 10–11.
20. Ibid., p. 5.
21. Details provided by Siddhi in Wimon, op. cit., pp. 101–112.
22. Ibid., pp. 12–13.
23. Krit Totsayanon, appendix D to Gilchrist, op. cit., pp. 213–221.
24. Smith and Clark, loc. cit.
25. Ibid., pp. 191–193.
26. Gilchrist, op. cit., p. 98.
27. U.S. Office of Strategic Services, Information Report Number Y5166 dated 15 March 1945, U.S. National Archives Document Number L54685, p. 1.
28. U.S. Department of the Army, op. cit., p. 17.
29. Gilchrist, op. cit., pp. 48–49.
30. Puay, op. cit., pp. 429–430.
31. Karawik, op. cit., p. 170.

32. Smith and Clark, op. cit., pp. 188–189.
33. U.S. War Department, op. cit., p. 412.
34. Malai, op. cit., p. 272.
35. U.S. War Department, op. cit., pp. 403–412.
36. Gilchrist, op. cit., p. 98.
37. This is based on my own personal research.
38. Smith and Clark, op. cit., pp. 193–196.

CHAPTER FIVE: BUILDING THE RESISTANCE BASE, 1942–1945

1. Malai, op. cit., p. 45.
2. Net, *Work*, op. cit., p. 513.
3. Malai, op. cit., pp. 262–264.
4. Ibid., pp. 391–393.
5. Ibid., pp. 345–346.
6. Lucy Starling, *Dawn Over Temple Roofs* (New York: World Horizons, Inc., 1960), pp. 159–160.
7. Elizabeth P. MacDonald, *Undercover Girl* (New York: The Macmillan Company, 1947), p. 10.
8. Jumsai, op. cit., p. 266; Malai, op. cit., pp. 391–395.
9. War Department, op. cit., p. 408.
10. Ibid.
11. Ibid.
11. Jumsai, op. cit., p. 271.
12. Smith and Clark, op. cit., p. 215.
13. Malai, op. cit., p. 365.
14. Thawi, op. cit., pp. 370–371.
15. U.S. Office of Strategic Services, *Political Aspects of an Allied Occupation of Thailand*, Research & Analysis Document No. 2114, dated 14 July 1944, p. 10.
16. Kelly, "Mission to Bangkok," op. cit., p. 93.
17. Phichet, op. cit., p. 21.
18. U.S. War Department, op. cit., pp. 17–18.
19. Ibid., pp. 20–25.
20. U.S. Department of the Army, *Thailand Operations Record*, op. cit., pp. 17–18.
21. Smith and Clark, op. cit., p. 284.
22. U.S. Department of State, *Foreign Relations, 1944, Volume V*, Washington, D.C.: Government Printing Office, 1945, p. 1312.

23. Ibid., pp. 1313–1314.
24. Ibid.
25. Ibid., pp. 1316–1317.
26. Ibid., pp. 1318–1319.
27. Direk, op. cit., pp. 321–325.
28. Gilchrist, op. cit., pp. 85–86.
29. Kelly, "Mission to Bangkok," op. cit., p. 90.
30. Smith and Clark, op. cit., pp. 199–200; Malai, op. cit., pp. 299–301.
31. Smith and Clark, Ibid., p. 200.
32. Gilchrist, op. cit., p. 128.
33. Direk, loc. cit.
34. Ibid., pp. 295–296.
35. Ibid., pp. 295–296.
36. Karawik, loc. cit.; Malai, op. cit., pp. 282–283.
37. Puay, loc. cit., pp. 429–430.
38. Krit, loc. cit.
39. Anthony Leviero, "Siam's Underground Foiled Enemy, Aided Our Free Access to Bangkok," *New York Times* (9 January 1946), p. 8.
40. Smith and Clark, op. cit., pp. 208–214.
41. Richard M. Kelly, "The Chance Island," Blue Book (March 1946), pp. 64–69.
42. Ibid., pp. 71–72.
43. Gilchrist, op. cit., pp. 112–120.
44. Ibid., p. 20.
45. Smith and Clark, op. cit., pp. 199–200.
46. Net, *Work*, op. cit., pp. 196–200; 218–220.

CHAPTER SIX: CONSOLIDATION, WAR PLANS, AND VICTORY, 1945

1. U.S. War Department, op. cit., p. 410.
2. Malai, op. cit., pp. 268–269.
3. Ibid., p. 327.
4. Malai, pp. 309–310.
5. Ibid., pp. 360–362.
6. Martin, op. cit., p. 463.
7. Smith and Clark, op. cit., p. 280.
8. Malai, pp. 363–364.

9. Thawi, op. cit., pp. 369–370.

10. Malai, op. cit., pp. 328–330.

11. Chiap (Chaisong) Amphunan, *Mahawitayalai Khong Khapachao* [My University] (Bangkok: Hang Hun Sam, Inc., 1957), pp. 149–150.

12. Thawi, op. cit., p. 371.

13. Smith and Clark, op. cit., pp. 208; 254–255.

14. Malai, op. cit., pp. 391–392; Smith and Clark, ibid., p. 281.

15. Kemp, Peter, *Arms for Oblivion* (London: Cassell and Company, 1961), pp. 11–18.

16. Karawik, op. cit., p. 178.

17. Thawi, op. cit., p. 369.

18. Phichet, op. cit., pp. 6–7.

19. Loftus, loc. cit.

20. U.S. Office of Strategic Services, Information Report Number 2M-1038 dated 8 May 1945, U.S. National Archives Document Number 126742, p. 1.

21. Ibid.

22. Smith and Clark, op. cit., pp. 215–216.

23. Kelly, "Mission to Bangkok," op. cit., p. 94.

24. Lieutenant Colonel Corey Ford, *Donovan of OSS* (Boston: Little, Brown and Company, 1970), p. 264; see also Smith and Clark, op. cit., pp. 190–191.

25. Thawi Chunlasap, op. cit., pp. 148–150.

26. Martin, loc. cit.

27. Nuechterlein, op. cit., p. 80.

28. Puay, op. cit., p. 427.

29. Gilchrist, op. cit., pp. 155–158.

30. Net, *Work*, op. cit., pp. 289–290.

31. Thawi Chunlasap, op. cit., pp. 65–71.

32. Ibid., pp. 998–1009.

33. Malai, op. cit., pp. 333–335.

34. Ibid., pp. 339–340.

35. Ibid., pp. 322–323.

36. Ibid., p. 303.

37. Edgar Snow, "Secrets from Siam," *Saturday Evening Post* 218 (12 January 1946), p. 371.

38. Karawik, op. cit., p. 169.

39. Loftus, loc. cit.

40. Herbert A. Fine, "The Liquidation of World War II in Thailand," *Pacific Historical Review* 34 (1965), pp. 69–70.

41. Malai, op. cit., pp. 353–356.

42. Smith and Clark, op. cit., p. 204.

43. Ibid., pp. 208–223.

44. Prida Dantrakun, *San Kadi Kan Mueang Nayok Mhuang Kap Me Thap Yipun* [An Account of the Politics of Prime Minister Khuang with the Japanese Commander in Chief] (Bangkok: Yim Seri Printing Company, 1949), p. 112.

45. Ibid., pp. 113–124.

46. Malai, op. cit., pp. 310–311.

47. Thawi Bunyaket, op. cit., p. 371.

48. Smith and Clark, op. cit., p. 284.

49. Jumsai, loc. cit.

50. U.S. Department of the Army, *Thailand Operations Record*, op. cit., pp. 24–27.

51. Malai, op. cit., p. 368.

52. Thawi Bunyaket, op. cit., p. 375.

53. Malai, op. cit., pp. 277–278.

BIBLIOGRAPHY

Blanchard, Wendell et al. *Thailand, Its People, Its Society, Its Culture.* New Haven, Conn.: Human Relations Area Files, Inc., 1958.

Chamkat Palangkun. *Free Thai Movement.* Report prepared for transmission to the OSS. 1943.

Charun Kuwanon. *Chiwit Kan To Su Khong Chomphon P. Phibulsongkhram* [The Fighting Life of Marshal P. Phibulsongkhram]. Bangkok: Akson Charoenthat Press, 1953.

Chiap (Chaisong) Amphunan. *Mahawitayalai Khong Khapachao* [My University]. Bangkok: 1957.

Darling, Frank C. *Thailand and the United States.* Washington, D.C:. Public Affairs Press, 1965.

Direk Chaiyanam. *Thai Kap Songkhram Lok Khrang Thi Song* [Thailand and World War II]. Bangkok: Prae Pittaya Press, 1966.

Fine, Herbert A. "The Liquidation of World War II in Thailand." *Pacific Historical Review* 34 (1965).

Fitzmaurice, Walter. "Thailand, Ally in Secret, Snooped Under Japs' Noses." *Newsweek* 26, 3 September 1945.

Ford, Lieutenant Colonel Corey. *Donovan of OSS.* Boston: Little, Brown and Company, 1970.

Gilchrist, Sir Andrew. *Bangkok Top Secret.* London: Hutchinson Publishers, 1970.

Jumsai, Brigadier General M.L. Manich. *History of Anglo-Thai Relations.* Bangkok: Chalermnit Press, 1970.

Karawik Chakrabandhu, M.C. "Force 136 and the Siamese Resistance Movement." *Asiatic Review* 43 (April 1947).

Kelly, Richard M. "The Chance Island." *Blue Book,* March 1946.

―――. "Mission to Bangkok." *Blue Book* , December 1946.

Kemp, Peter. *Arms for Oblivion*. London: Cassell and Company, 1961.

Krit Totsayanon. "Appendix D." In *Bangkok Top Secret*, by Sir Andrew Gilchrist (London: Hutchinson Publishers, 1970).

Landon, Margaret. "Thailand Under the Japanese." *Asia and the Americas* 44 (September 1944).

Leviero, Anthony. "Siam's Underground Foiled Enemy, Aided Our Free Access to Bangkok." *New York Times*, 9 January 1946.

Loftus, Joseph A. "Secret Thai Role in War Detailed." *New York Times*, 9 September 1945, Section II.

MacDonald, Elizabeth P. *Undercover Girl.* New York: The Macmillan Company, 1947.

Malai Chuphanit (pseudonym Chanthana). *X. O. Group*. Bangkok: Khao Na Printers, 1964.

Martin, James V. Jr. "Thai-American Relations in World War II." *Journal of Asian Studies* 21 (August 1963).

Miles, Vice Admiral Milton E. *A Different Kind of War*. Garden City, N.Y.: Doubleday, 1967.

General Net Khemayothin. *Chiwit Khong Naiphon* [A General's Life]. Bangkok: Fuang Akson Press, 1967.

―――. *Ngan Tai Din Khong Pan Ek Yothi* [The Underground Work of Colonel Yothi]. Bangkok: Fuang Akson Press, 1967.

Nuechterlein, Donald E. *Thailand and the Struggle for Southeast Asia*. Ithaca, N.Y.: Cornell University Press, 1965.

Phichet, Colonel S. *Siam in World War II, A Description of the Japanese Invasion of Siam and the Effort of the People in Resistance Activities*. Unpublished paper presented to the Regular course of the U.S. Army Command and General Staff College, Fort Leavenworth, Kans., 1947.

Prida Dantrakun. *San Khadi Kan Mueang Nayok Khuang Kap Me Thap Yipun* [An Account of the Politics of Prime Minister Khuang with the Japanese Commander in Chief]. Bangkok: Yim Seri Printing Company, 1949.

Pridi Banomyong. Speech in Bangkok on 26 September 1945, reported to OSS in OSS Memorandum B-27 dated 6 October 1945, U.S. National Archives Document Number XL24262.

Puay Ungphakon. "*Thahan Chuakhrao* [Temporary Soldier]." In *Thai Kap Songkhram Lok Khrang Thi Song* [Thailand and World War II] by Direk Chaiyanam (Bangkok: Prae Pittaya Press, 1966).

Quaritch-Wales, H. C. "Thailand—Key to the Coming Attack on Japan." *Asia and the Americas* 42 (September 1942).

Ray, Jayanta Kumar. *Portraits of Thai Politics.* New Delhi: Orient Longman, Ltd., 1972.

Nai Samrej (a pseudonym of an unidentified senior Thai official). "That Thailand May Be Free." *Asia and the Americas* 45 (February 1945), pp. 94–95.

M.R. Seni Pramoj. "Relationship Between Thailand and the U.S.A. during the Second World War." Lecture delivered at Chulalongkorn University, Bangkok, on 17 August 1946, contained in a private printing of M.R. Seni's works.

————. Manuscript of a speech given 17 August 1946, unpaged.

Smith, Nicol and Blake Clark. *Into Siam, Underground Kingdom.* New York: Bobbs Merrill Company, 1945.

Smith, R. Harris. *OSS: The Secret History of America's First Central Intelligence Agency.* Berkeley, Calif.: University of California Press, 1972.

Snow, Edgar. "Secrets from Siam." *Saturday Evening Post* 218, 12 January 1946.

Starling, Lucy. *Dawn Over Temple Roofs.* New York: World Horizons, Inc., 1960.

Thawi Bunyaket. "Thai Kap Songkhram Lok Khrang Thi Song" [Thailand and World War II]. Appendix to Direk Chaiyanam's work of the same name, 1966.

Air Chief Marshal Thawi Chunlasap. *Chat Yu Nuea Sing Dai* [My Country Above All]. Bangkok: privately published, 1974.

U.S. Department of the Army. *Field Manual 31-21: Special Forces Operations, U.S. Army Doctrine,* 20 December 1974. Washington, D.C.: Headquarters Department of the Army, 1974.

U.S. Department of the Army. *Thailand Operations Record, Japanese Monograph #177,* Tokyo: Headquarters Army Forces Far East, 1953.

U.S. Department of State. *Foreign Relations, 1944.* Vol. 5. Washington, D.C.: Government Printing Office, 1945.

U.S. Office of Strategic Services. "Escape of Allied Airmen from the Kra Isthmus." OSS Memorandum Number K-90 dated 21 April 1945, U.S. National Archives Document Number 126742.

U.S. Office of Strategic Services. Information Report Number 2M-1038 dated 8 May 1945, U.S. National Archives Document Number 12674.

U.S. Office of Strategic Services, Information Report Number Y5166 dated 15 March 1945, U.S. National Archives Document Number L54685.

U.S. Office of Strategic Services. *Political Aspects of an Allied Occupation of Thailand.* Research & Analysis Document Number 2114, dated 14 July 1944.

U.S. War Department. *War Report: Office of Strategic Services (OSS), Volume 2 (Operations).* Washington, D.C.: Government Printing Office, 1949.

Luang Wichit Wathakan. Text in *Behind the Declaration of War* (1947), a privately published edition of Wichit's works translated into English. Bangkok, 1967.

Wilasuang Phongsabut. *Prawatisat Thai* [History of Thailand]. Bangkok: Thai Wattana Printing Company, Inc., 1976.

Wimon Wiriyawit. *Free Thai.* Bangkok: White Lotus Press, 1997.

INDEX